knitting beyond the edge

cuffs & collars • necklines • corners & edges • closures

knitting beyond the edge

cuffs & collars • necklines • corners & edges • closures

the essential collection of decorative finishes

nicky epstein

author of *Knitting On the Edge* and *Knitting Over the Edge*

sixth&spring books

To my Aunts—who have shared their hearts, wisdom, and recipes with me all my life.

sixth&spring
books

Editorial Director
TRISHA MALCOLM

Art Director
CHI LING MOY

Book Division Manager
ERICA SMITH

Executive Editor
CARLA SCOTT

Associate Editor
ERIN WALSH

Instructions Editors
LISA BUCCELLATO
RITA GREENFEDER
EVE NG
CHARLOTTE PARRY

Instructions Proofreader
NANCY HENDERSON

Technical Illustrations
ULI MÖNCH

Graphic Designer
SHEENA T. PAUL

Production Manager
DAVID JOINNIDES

Photography
JACK DEUTSCH STUDIOS

President, Sixth&Spring Books
ART JOINNIDES

Library of Congress Control Number: 2006924833
ISBN: 1-933027-01-0
ISBN 13: 978-1-933027-01-2

1 3 5 7 9 10 8 6 4 2
Manufactured in China

First Edition

contents

introduction	7
notes	8
neckline variations	9
cuffs & collars	12
necklines	56
corners & edges	78
closures	110
patterns	136
necklines & patterns	148
adjusting your edge	151
terms & abbreviations	152
stitches	153
techniques	154
acknowledgments	155
resources	157

introduction

When I began writing *Knitting On the Edge* three years ago, I had no idea I was embarking upon such a long voyage.
To my surprise, the book was successful beyond anything I had expected. Prompted by that success,
I wrote *Knitting Over The Edge*. The public response to that book was so overwhelmingly positive, that now—
three years, more than 900 edgings, and countless hours later—I've completed the trilogy with *Knitting Beyond the Edge*.

The journey has been intense, enlightening and exhilarating. As I travel around the world, students, designers, readers and
knitters of all skills tell me how the books have inspired their creativity and added a whole new dimension to their work.
People everywhere have told me how these edging books help them think "outside the box." Some even consider them
indispensable. These unsolicited expressions of support have made my journey a most rewarding one.

Knitting Beyond the Edge explores new territory: cuffs and collars using stitch patterns, lace, ribs, cords in a variety of styles;
closures that include unusual buttonhole treatments, frog cords and button bands; corners and angles with unique stitch
patterns and shapings; and new ways to use knit leaves, bobbles, flowers and purchased pieces such as trims and
buttons as embellishments.

The garments in this book range from easy to intricate. The novice knitter will enjoy making the Deep V Ruffle Pullover, while
more experienced knitters will find satisfying projects in the Belle Epoque Jacket, Cardigan with Cabled Points, Faux Fair Isle
Jacket and the Hooded Shawl.

I hope these books give your work new scope, style and individuality. Knitting is fun, so have fun and keep knitting on, over and
beyond the edge.

Nicky Epstein

notes on using this book

I am often asked, "How can I use these edgings? Do I have to sew them on after the piece is knit? Do I knit them from the bottom up or the top down? How can I figure out how many stitches I need?"

In this book, I am not only giving you the edgings alone, but I am giving you examples of what they actually look like once applied to a neck edge, cuff or front band of a cardigan. Refer to "adjusting your edge" (page 151) as a guide to customizing your garment. Note the section on "necklines & patterns" (page 148). This section gives you instructions on seven basic necklines on which you can apply any of the edgings.

There are several ways to create edgings: knitting from the bottom up, knitting from the top down, or knitting separately, then turning the edging horizontally in order to pick up stitches along the selvage edge or sewing onto the main piece. In most of the instructions, we have used the symbols shown below to indicate the direction in which the edging was knit. In many cases, the edgings in this book are reversible.

▲ Knit from bottom up: Cast-on edge is the lower edge.

▼ Knit from the top down: Bound-off edge is the lower edge.

▶ Knit separately: Stitches can be picked up or sewn on.

◀▶ Reversible: Both sides are the same or equally attractive.

▶▲ Knit separately: stitches are joined together onto one needle, sometimes adding stitches in between, then the edging continues upward.

▼ ▶▲ The center is worked separately, then encased by picking up stitches along bottom and top and working in either direction.

▲▶ Knit vertically, then sewn on or picked up and knit horizontally.

Standard Yarn Weights

In the Patterns chapter, next to the suggested yarn in the Materials section, we have used the Standard Yarn Weight System for ease in substitution. If you plan to substitute a yarn, be sure to knit a gauge swatch and check that it matches the original gauge in the pattern and has a similar appearance to the original yarn used in the pattern. These standard yarn weights can be used for any pattern.

A helpful hint: Many of the edgings, whether knitted from the bottom up, top down or sideways, can be made separately and then sewn on to any piece. They can also be layered with the Three-needle Joining method (one of my favorite techniques) and I have used it in this book several times (see page 152).

For notes on constructing necklines, see page 148.

For descriptions and illustrations of stitches, see page 153.

For techniques on basic buttonholes, cord buttons, making cords and rib flap love knots, see page 154.

For terms and abbreviations used in this book, see page 156.

Standard Yarn Weight System

Categories of yarn, gauge ranges, and recommended needle and hook sizes

Yarn Weight Symbol & Category Names	1 Super Fine	2 Fine	3 Light	4 Medium	5 Bulky	6 Super Bulky
Type of Yarns in Category	Sock, Fingering, Baby	Sport, Baby	DK, Light Worsted	Worsted, Afghan, Aran	Chunky, Craft, Rug	Bulky, Roving
Knit Gauge Range* in Stockinette Stitch to 4 Inches	27–32 sts	23–26 sts	21–24 sts	16–20 sts	12–15 sts	6–11 sts
Recommended Needle in Metric Size Range	2.25–3.25 mm	3.25–3.75 mm	3.75–4.5 mm	4.5–5.5 mm	5.5–8 mm	8 mm and larger
Recommended Needle U.S. Size Range	1 to 3	3 to 5	5 to 7	7 to 9	9 to 11	11 and larger

*Guidelines only: The above reflect the most commonly used gauges and needle sizes for specific yarn categories.

rib flap necklines

Using your imagination, a basic neckline can be
reconstructed in many different ways. Here is one set
of variations you can do with simple rib flaps.

1 rib flaps

▶▲ Cast on 7 sts.

Row 1 *K1, p1; rep from *, end k1.

Row 2 *P1, k1; rep from *, end p1.

Rep rows 1 and 2 for 25 rows (work 24 rows for version 6).

Break yarn, leave on needle.

With free needle, cast on 7 sts and rep for desired number
of flaps.

Connecting row *Work 7 sts of one flap on LH needle,
cast on 1 st; rep from * to last flap, work 7 sts.

Cont in k1, p1 rib to desired length of collar allowing for fold.

Bind off. Sew bound-off edge to connecting row.

2 loop flaps

▶▲ Sew cast on edge of first flap behind second flap.
Rep this across all flaps. Sew last flap into seam.

3 knot flaps

▶▲ Knot each set of two flaps together and tack the
cast-on edges together.

4 button flaps

▶▲ Fold flaps to RS and sew on buttons.

5 end knot flaps

▶▲ Make a knot at end of each flap.

6 love knot flaps

▶▲ Work to connecting row, then knot two flaps
together for each set using a love knot
(see page 154 for technique).

7 top knot flaps

▶▲ Make a knot at upper part of each flap.

cuffs &

collars

arches and columns collar

▲ Cast on 141 sts.

Work in arches and columns pattern for 7"/18 cm.

Next row (RS) K3, [k2tog] to end—72 sts.

Work in St st for 1"/2.5cm.

Purl 1 row on RS for turning ridge.

Purl next row.

Work in St st for 1"/2.5cm for facing.

Bind off.

Fold facing to wrong side along turning ridge and sew to inside edge.

Attach a 20"/51cm piece of 1"/2.5cm wide ribbon to each edge of St st.

arches and columns pattern

(multiple of 14 sts plus 1)

Rows 1 and 3 (WS) Purl.

Row 2 K2tog, yo, *k3, yo, k1, SK2P, k1, yo, k3, yo, SK2P, yo; rep from *, end k3, yo, k1, SK2P, k1, yo, k3, yo, ssk.

Row 4 K2tog, yo, *k4, yo, SK2P, yo; rep from *, end k4, yo, ssk.

Rep rows 1–4.

star rib mesh collar

▲ Cast on 189 sts.

Work in star rib mesh pattern for 3½"/9 cm.

Next row (RS) K3tog to end—63 sts.

Work k1, p1 rib for 1"/2.5cm.

Bind off.

star rib mesh pattern

(multiple of 4 sts plus 1)

Rows 1 and 3 (WS) Purl.

Row 2 K1, *yo, [sl 2 knitwise, k1, p2sso], yo, k1; rep from * to end.

Row 4 Ssk, yo, k1, *yo, [sl 2 knitwise, k1, p2sso], yo, k1; rep from *, end yo, k2tog.

Rep rows 1–4.

dainty chevron collar

▲ Cast on 217 sts.

Knit 2 rows.

Work in dainty chevron pattern for 2½"/6.5cm.

Next row (RS) *[K3tog] twice, [sl 2, k2tog, p2sso]; rep from *, end k3tog, [sl2, k2tog, p2sso]—65 sts.

Purl next row.

Work in St st for 2"/5cm.

Bind off.

Sew a bead to each point on row 6 and row 10.

dainty chevron pattern

(multiple of 8 sts plus 1)

Row 1 and all WS rows Purl.

Rows 2 and 4 K1, *ssk, [k1, yo] twice, k1, k2tog, k1; rep from * to end.

Row 6 K1, *yo, ssk, k3, k2tog, yo, k1; rep from * to end.

Row 8 K2, *yo, ssk, k1, k2tog, yo, k3; rep from *, end last rep k2.

Row 10 K3, *yo, [sl 2, k1, p2sso], yo, k5; rep from *, end last rep k3.

Rep rows 1–10.

petite chevron collar

▲ Cast on 217 sts.

Knit 2 rows.

Work in petite chevron pattern for 1¾"/4.5cm.

Next row (RS) *[K3tog] twice, [sl 2, k2tog, p2sso]; rep from *, end k3tog, [sl 2, k2tog, p2sso]—65 sts.

Purl next row.

Work in k1, p1 rib for 1"/2.5cm.

Bind off.

petite chevron pattern

(multiple of 8 sts plus 1)

Row 1 (RS) K1, *ssk, [k1, yo] twice, k1, k2tog, k1; rep from * to end.

Row 2 P1, *p2tog, [p1, yo] twice, p1, p2tog tbl, p1; rep from * to end.

Row 3 K1, *yo, ssk, k3, k2tog, yo, k1; rep from * to end.

Row 4 P2, *yo, p2tog, p1, p2tog tbl, yo, p3; rep from *, end last rep p2.

Row 5 K3, *yo, [sl 2, k1, p2sso], yo, k5; rep from *, end last rep k3.

Row 6 Rep row 2.

Row 7 Rep row 1.

Row 8 P1, *yo, p2tog, p3, p2tog tbl, yo, p1; rep from * to end.

Row 9 K2, *yo, ssk, k1, k2tog, yo, k3; rep from *, end last rep k2.

Row 10 P3, *yo, [sl 2, p1, p2sso], yo, p5, rep from *, end last rep p3.

Rep rows 1–10.

bird's eye collar

▲ Cast on 192 sts.

Knit 2 rows.

Work in bird's eye pattern for 2"/5cm.

Next row (RS) K3tog to end—64 sts.

Purl next row.

Work in St st for 1"/2.5cm.

Eyelet row (RS) K1, *k2tog, yo; rep from *, end k1.

Purl next row.

Work in St st for 1"/2.5cm for facing.

Bind off.

Fold facing to wrong side along eyelet row and sew to inside edge.

bird's eye pattern

(multiple of 4 sts)

Row 1 (WS) *K2tog, [yo] twice, k2tog; rep from * to end.

Row 2 *K1, [k1, p1] into double yo, k1; rep from * to end.

Row 3 K2, *k2tog, [yo] twice, k2tog; rep from *, end k2.

Row 4 K2, *k1, [k1, p1] into double yo, k1; rep from *, end k2.

Rep rows 1–4.

vertical drop-stitch collar

▲ Cast on 188 sts.

Knit 2 rows.

Work in vertical drop-stitch pattern for one repeat.

Next row (WS) P3tog across to last 2 sts, p2—64 sts.

Knit next row.

Work in St st for 1"/2.5 cm.

Purl 1 row on RS for turning ridge.

Purl next row.

Work in St st for 1"/2.5cm for facing.

Bind off.

Fold facing to wrong side along turning ridge and sew to inside edge.

Sew a pearl in each dropped stitch along row 1.

vertical drop-stitch pattern

(beg with a multiple of 8 sts plus 4)

Preparation row (RS) K1, *p2, k1, yo, k1, p2, k2; rep from *, end p2, k1.

Rows 1, 3, and 5 (WS) P1, *k2, p2, k2, p3; rep from *, end k2, p1.

Rows 2 and 4 K1, *p2, k3, p2, k2; rep from *, end p2, k1.

Row 6 K1, *p2, k1, drop next st off needle and unravel down to the yo 6 rows below, k1, p2, k1, yo, k1; rep from *, end p2, k1.

Rows 7, 9, and 11 P1, *k2, p3, k2, p2; rep from *, end k2, p1.

Rows 8 and 10 K1, *p2, k2, p2, k3; rep from *, end p2, k1.

Row 12 K1, *p2, k1, yo, k1, p2, k1, drop next st off needle and unravel down to the yo 6 rows below, k1; rep from *, end p2, k1.

Rep rows 1–12.

gable cuff

▲ Cast on 42 sts.

Work 28 rows in gable pattern.

Cont in St st.

Attach a small ribbon bow to each pat rep on row 1.

gable pattern

(multiple of 10 sts plus 2)

LT Skip first st on LH needle and knit the second stitch tbl.

Then knit the first st and slip both off of LH needle.

RT Skip first st on LH needle and knit the second st.

Then knit the first st and slip both off of LH needle.

Row 1 (RS) K4, *RT, LT, k1, ssk, yo, k3; rep from *, end last rep k1.

Row 2 P9, *p2tog, yo, p8; rep from *, end p2tog, yo, p1.

Row 3 K3, *RT, k2, LT, k4; rep from *, end last rep k3.

Row 4 Purl.

Row 5 K2, *RT, k4, LT, k2; rep from * to end.

Row 6 P4, *p2tog, yo, p8; rep from *, end last rep p6.

Row 7 K1, *RT, k1, ssk, yo, k3, LT; rep from *, end k1.

Rows 8, 10, 12 and 14 K2, *p2, p2tog, yo, p4, k2; rep from * to end.

Rows 9, 11 and 13 P2, *k2, ssk, yo, k4, p2; rep from * to end.

Row 15 K1, *LT, k1, ssk, yo, k3, RT; rep from *, end k1.

Rows 16, 18 and 20 Rep rows 6, 4 and 2.

Row 17 K2, *LT, k4, RT, k2; rep from * to end.

Row 19 K3, *LT, k2, RT, k4; rep from *, end last rep k3.

Row 21 K4, *LT, RT, k1, ssk, yo, k3; rep from *, end last rep k1.

Rows 22, 24, 26 and 28 P5, *k2, p2, p2tog, yo, p4; rep from *,
end last rep p1.

Rows 23, 25 and 27 K5, *p2, k2, ssk, yo, k4; rep from *, end last rep k1.

Rep rows 1–28.

& collars

sea scallop edge cuff

▲ Cast on 44 sts.

Work in sea scallop edge pattern for 2½"/6.5 cm.

Cont in St st.

Make 4 bobbles (see page 152) and attach to every eleventh st.

sea scallop edge pattern

(multiple of 11 sts)

Row 1 (RS) Knit.

Rows 2 and 4 Purl.

Row 3 *[P2tog] twice, [M1, k1] 3 times, M1, [p2tog] twice;
rep from * to end.

Rows 5 and 6 Knit.

Row 7 *[K2, p2] twice, k1, p2; rep from * to end.

Row 8 *K2, p1, [k2, p2] twice; rep from * to end.

Rep rows 7 and 8 for rib until desired length.

pillar and web cuff

▲ Cast on 122 sts.

Knit 2 rows.

Work in pillar and web pattern for 2½"/6.5cm.

Next row (RS) K1, *k3tog; rep from *,
end k1—42 sts.

Cont in k1, p1 rib.

Sew a bead to each scallop on pat row 1.

pillar and web pattern

(multiple of 6 sts plus 2)

Note 2 needle sizes are used, one
needle 4 sizes larger than the other.

Row 1 (WS) With larger needle, knit.

Row 2 With smaller needle, k1,
*(skip 3 sts and purl the 4th st,
drawing it off needle over the 3
skipped sts) 3 times, then purl the 3
skipped sts; rep from *, end k1.

Rep rows 1 and 2.

sea foam cuff

▲ Cast on 86 sts.

Work in sea foam pattern for 16 rows.

Next row (RS) K3, *k2tog, [k2tog, pass the first k2tog over the second k2tog]; rep from *, end k3—26 sts.

Purl next row.

Cont in St st.

sea foam collar

▲ Cast on 246 sts.

Work in sea foam pattern for 16 rows.

Next row (RS) K3, *k2tog, k2tog, pass the first k2tog over the second k2to]; rep from *, end k3—66 sts.

Purl next row.

Work in St st for 2½"/6.5 cm.

Bind off.

sea foam pattern

(multiple of 10 sts plus 6)

Rows 1 and 2 Knit.

Row 3 (RS) K6, *[yo] twice, k1, [yo] 3 times, k1, [yo] 4 times, k1, [yo] 3 times, k1, [yo] twice, k6; rep from * to end.

Row 4 Knit, dropping all yo's off needle.

Rows 5 and 6 Knit.

Row 7 K1, rep from * of row 3, end last rep k1.

Row 8 Rep row 4.

Rep rows 1–8.

dimple stitch cuff

▲ Cast on 47 sts.

Work in dimple stitch pattern for 2½"/6.5cm, end with row 1 or 9.

Cont in St st.

If desired, sew small pearls at each pat intersection.

dimple stitch pattern

(multiple of 6 sts plus 5)

Row 1 (WS) Knit.

Rows 2 and 4 K1, *sl 3 wyif, p3; rep from *, end sl 3 wyif, k1.

Row 3 K1, *sl 3 wyib, k3, rep from *, end sl 3 wyib, k1.

Rows 5 and 7 Knit.

Row 6 Purl.

Row 8 K1, p1, *insert needle from below under the 3 loose strands of rows 2, 3 and 4 and k next st, bringing st out under strands, p5; rep from *, end last rep p1, k1.

Row 9 Knit.

Rows 10 and 12 K1, *p3, sl 3 wyif; rep from *, end p3, k1.

Row 11 K4, *sl 3 wyib, k3; rep from *, end k1.

Rows 13 and 15 Knit.

Row 14 Purl.

Row 16 K1, p4, *knit next st under 3 loose strands of rows 10, 11, and 12, p5; rep from *, end last rep p4, k1.

Rep rows 1–16.

royal ruffle cuff

▲ With B, cast on 99 sts.

Knit 2 rows.

Work in royal ruffle pattern for 2"/5cm, end with row 4 or 8.

Next row (WS) With B, p3, [p2tog] to end—51 sts.

Knit next row.

Cont in St st.

royal ruffle pattern

(multiple of 6 sts plus 3)

Colors A and B

PU1 (Pick up 1) Insert point of RH needle upwards under the loose strand of the sl stitches 3 rows below and knit it together with the next stitch.

Preparation row (RS) Using A, knit.

Row 1 (WS) Using A, p2, *sl 5 wyib, p1; rep from * to last st, p1.

Row 2 Using B, knit.

Row 3 Using B, purl.

Row 4 Using A, k1, sl 3 wyib, PU1, *sl 5 wyib, PU1; rep from *, end sl 3 wyib, k1.

Row 5 Using A, p1, sl 3 wyib, p1, *sl 5 wyib, p1; rep from *, end sl 3 wyib, p1.

Row 6 Using B, knit.

Row 7 Using B, purl.

Row 8 Using A, k1, PU1, *sl 5 wyib, PU1; rep from *, end k1.

Rep rows 1–8.

& collars

suzie q cuff

▲ With A, cast on 50 sts.

Knit 2 rows.

Work in susie q pattern for 2"/5cm, end with row 4 or 8.

With A, cont in St st.

susie q pattern

(multiple of 6 sts plus 2)

Colors A and B

3-st LC Sl 1 st to cn and hold in front, k2, then k1 from cn.

3-st RC Sl 2 st to cn and hold in back, k1, then k2 from cn.

Row 1 (WS) With A, k1, p1, k4, *p2, k4; rep from *, end last rep p1, k1.

Row 2 With B, k1, sl 1, k4, *sl 2, k4; rep from *, end last rep sl 1, k1.

Row 3 With B, p1, sl 1, p4, *sl 2, p4; rep from * end last rep, sl 1, p1.

Row 4 With A, k1, *3-st LC, 3-st RC; rep from *, end k1.

Row 5 With A, k3, p2, *k4, p2; rep from *, end k3.

Row 6 With B, k3, sl 2, *k4, sl 2; rep from *, end k3.

Row 7 With B, p3, sl 2, *p4, sl 2; rep from * end p3.

Row 8 With A, k1, *3-st RC, 3-st LC; rep from *, end k1.

Rep rows 1–8.

bell sleeve cross stitch cuff

▲ **Colors** A and B

With A, cast on 53 sts.

Work in St st for 22 rows, dec 1 st each edge every 4th row 5 times—43 sts.

With B, cont in St st for 8 rows.

With A, cont in St st.

With A, embroider cross stitches over 4 sts and 4 rows of B.

cluster quilting cuff

▲ With B, cast on 113 sts.

With B, knit 2 rows.

With B, work in St st for 1"/2.5cm, end with row 5 or 11.

Next row (RS) With A, k1, *k2tog, k2tog, k3tog, pass 2nd k2tog over the k3tog; rep from * to end—33 sts.

Work in cluster quilting pattern for 4½"/11.5cm.

With B, cont in St st.

cluster quilting pattern

(multiple of 8 sts plus 1)

Colors A and B

Preparation row (WS) With A, p1, *p1 wrapping yarn twice, p5, p1 wrapping yarn twice, p1; rep from * to end.

Row 1 With B, k1, *sl 1 wyib dropping extra wrap, k5, sl 1 wyib dropping extra wrap, k1; rep from * to end.

Row 2 With B, p1, *sl 1 wyif, p5, sl 1 wyif, p1; rep from * to end.

Row 3 With B, k1, *sl 1 wyib, k5, sl 1 wyib, k1; rep from * to end.

Row 4 With B, purl, dropping all elongated sl sts off needle to front of work.

Row 5 With A, k1, sl 1 wyib, k1, *pick up first dropped st and k it, k1, pick up next dropped st and k it, then [wyib sl the last 3 sts worked back to LH needle, pass yarn to front, sl the same 3 sts back again to RH needle, pass yarn to back] twice, k1, sl 3 wyib, k1; rep from *, end last rep sl 1 wyib, k1.

Row 6 With A, p1, sl 1 wyif, *[p1, p1 wrapping yarn twice] twice, p1, sl 3 wyif; rep from *, end last rep sl 1 wyif.

Row 7 With B, k3, *sl 1 wyib dropping extra wrap, k1, sl 1 wyib dropping extra wrap, k5; rep from *, end last rep k3.

Row 8 With B, p3, *sl 1 wyif, p1, sl 1 wyif, p5; rep from *, end last rep p3.

Row 9 With B, k3, *sl 1 wyib, k1, sl 1 wyib, k5; rep from *, end last rep k3.

Row 10 With B, purl, dropping all elongated sl sts off needle to back.

Row 11 With A, k1, pick up first dropped st and k it, k1, sl 3 wyib, k1; rep from * of row 5, end pick up last dropped st and knit it, k1.

Row 12 With A, p1, *p1 wrapping yarn twice, p1, sl 3 wyif, p1, p1 wrapping yarn twice, p1; rep from * to end.

Rep rows 1–12.

banded crescent cuff

▲ Cast on 45 sts.

Work in banded crescent pattern for 24 rows.

Knit 6 rows.

Cont in St st.

Sew purchased lace to cuff edge.

banded crescent pattern

(multiple of 3 sts)

Row 1 (WS) Knit.

Rows 2 and 3 Purl.

Row 4 K2, *sl 1 wyib, k2; rep from *, end k1.

Row 5 P3, *sl 1 wyif, p2; rep from * to end.

Row 6 K2, *drop sl st off needle to front of work, k2, pick up dropped st and k it; rep from *, end k1.

Row 7 Purl.

Row 8 K2, *yo, k2tog, k1; rep from *, end k1.

Row 9 Purl.

Row 10 K4, *sl 1 wyib, k2; rep from *, end sl 1, k1.

Row 11 P1, *sl 1 wyif, p2; rep from *, end p2.

Row 12 K2, *sl 2 wyib, drop next sl st off needle to front of work, sl the same 2 sts back to LH needle, pick up dropped st and k it, k2; rep from *, end k1.

Rep rows 1–12.

slipped hourglass collar/cuff

collar

▲ Cast on 98 sts.

Knit 2 rows.

Work in slipped hourglass pattern for 20 rows.

Bind off.

Make Le Fleur (see page 154) and sew to each hourglass as shown.

Sew a bead to center of each flower.

cuff

▲ Cast on 50 sts.

Knit 2 rows.

Work in slipped hourglass pattern for 20 rows.

Cont in St st.

Make Le Fleur (see page 154) and sew to each hourglass as shown.

Sew a bead to center of each flower.

slipped hourglass pattern

(multiple of 8 sts plus 2)

2-st LPC Sl 1 st onto cn and hold to front, p1, then k1 from cn.

2-st RPC Sl 1 st onto cn and hold to back, k1, then p1 from cn.

Rows 1 and 3 (RS) P1, *p3, k2, p3; rep from *, end p1.

Row 2 and all WS rows Knit all knit sts, sl all purl sts wyif.

(Thus rows 2 and 4: K1, *k3, sl 2 wyif, k3; rep from *, end k1).

Row 5 P1, *p2, 2-st RPC, 2-st LPC, p2; rep from *, end p1.

Row 7 P1, *p1, 2-st RPC, p2, 2-st LPC, p1; rep from *, end p1.

Row 9 P1, *2-st RPC, p4, 2-st LPC; rep from *, end p1.

Rows 11 and 13 P1, *k1, p6, k1; rep from *, end p1.

Row 15 P1, *2-st LPC, p4, 2-st RPC; rep from *, end p1.

Row 17 P1, *p1, 2-st LPC, p2, 2-st RPC, p1; rep from *, end p1.

Row 19 P1, *p2, 2-st LPC, 2-st RPC, p2; rep from *, end p1.

Row 20 Knit all knit sts, sl all purl sts wyif.

Rep rows 1–20.

& collars

ribbed leaf cuff

▲ Cast on 49 sts.

Work in ribbed leaf pattern for 28 rows.

Cont in St st.

Sew purchased flower to center of ribbed leaf pat.

ribbed leaf pattern

▲ (multiple of 16 sts plus 1)

Row 1 and all WS rows Purl.

Row 2 K1, *LT, [RT] twice, k3, [LT] twice, RT, k1; rep from * to end.

Row 4 K2, *LT, [RT] twice, k1, [LT] twice, RT, k3; rep from *, end last rep k2.

Row 6 K1, *[LT] twice, RT, k3, LT, [RT] twice, k1; rep from * to end.

Row 8 K2, *[LT] twice, RT, k1, LT, [RT] twice, k3; rep from *, end last rep k2.

Row 10 K1, *[LT] 3 times, k3, [RT] 3 times, k1; rep from * to end.

Row 12 K2, *[LT] 3 times, k1, [RT] 3 times, k3; rep from *, end last rep k2.

Rows 14, 16, 18, 20 and 22 Rep rows 10, 8, 6, 4, and 2.

Row 24 K2, *[RT] 3 times, k1, [LT] 3 times, k3; rep from *, end last rep k2.

Row 26 K1, *[RT] 3 times, k3, [LT] 3 times, k1; rep from * to end.

Row 28 Rep row 24.

Rep rows 1–28.

LT Skip first st on LH needle and knit the second stitch tbl.
Then knit the first st and slip both off of LH needle.
RT Skip first st on LH needle and knit the second st.
Then knit the first st and slip both off of LH needle.

fractured lattice cuff

▲ Cast on 48 sts.

Work in fractured lattice pattern for 16 rows.

Cont in St st.

Sew a purchased bead tassel to center.

fractured lattice pattern

(multiple of 8 sts)

Row 1 and all WS rows Purl.

Row 2 *LT, k2, LT, RT; rep from * to end.

Row 4 K1, *LT, k2, RT, k2; rep from *, end last rep k1.

Row 6 *RT, LT, RT, k2; rep from * to end.

Row 8 K3, *LT, k2, RT, k2; rep from *, end LT, k3.

Rep rows 1–8.

bamboo rib collar/cuff

collar

▲▶ Cast on 30 sts.

Work in bamboo rib pattern for 15"/38cm
or desired length for neck.

Bind off.

cuff

▲▶ Cast on 30 sts.

Work in bamboo rib pattern for 8"/20cm
or desired length for wrist.

Bind off.

bamboo rib pattern

(worked over 30 sts)

Rows 1, 3, and 5 (RS) K5, [p2, k4] 3 times,
p2, k5.

Rows 2, 4, and 6 P5, k2, [p4, k2] 3 times, p5.

Row 7 K1, [p4, k2] 4 times, p4, k1.

Row 8 P1, k 4, [p2, k4] 4 times, p1.

Rows 9 and 10 Rep rows 1 and 2.

Rep rows 1–10.

horizontal triple bobble collar/cuff

collar

▲ Cast on 97 sts.

Work in horizontal triple bobble pattern for 14 rows.

Cont in k1, p1 rib for 3"/7.6cm.

Bind off.

Fold rib to wrong side and sew to first rib row.

cuff

▲ Cast on 49 sts.

Work in horizontal triple bobble pattern for 14 rows.

Cont in k1, p1 rib.

horizontal triple bobble pattern

(multiple of 4 sts plus 1)

MB (Make bobble) ([K1, p1] twice, k1) in same st—5 sts made, turn, k5, turn, p5, turn, k5, sl 2nd, 3rd, 4th, and 5th st over first st, turn, k1.

Rows 1 and 2 Knit.

Row 3 (RS) K2, *MB, k3; rep from *, end last rep MB, k2.

Rows 4 and 6 K2, p to last 2 sts, k2.

Row 5 Knit.

Rep rows 3–6.

open spoke bobble collar/cuff

collar

▲ Cast on 97 sts.

Work in open spoke bobble pattern for 2½"/6.5cm.

Work in reverse St st for 3 rows.

Bind off. Edge will curl to wrong side.

Make bobbles (see page 152) and sew to each point on row 1.

cuff

▲ Cast on 49 sts.

Work in open spoke bobble pattern for 2½"/6.5cm.

Cont in reverse St st.

Make bobbles (see page 152) and sew to each point on row 1.

open spoke bobble pattern

(multiple of 12 sts plus 1)

Rows 1, 3 and 5 (WS) K1, *yo, k4, p3tog, k4, yo, k1; rep from * to end.

Rows 2, 4 and 6 K1, *yo, p4, p3tog, p4, yo, k1; rep from * to end.

Rows 7, 9 and 11 P2tog, *k4, yo, k1, yo, k4, p3tog; rep from *,
end last rep p2tog.

Rows 8, 10 and 12 P2tog, *p4, yo, k1, yo, p4, p3tog; rep from *,
end last rep p2tog.

Rep rows 1–12.

& collars

lace puff bobble cuff

▲ Cast on 50 sts.

Work in lace puff pattern for 32 rows.

Cont in St st.

Make bobble (see page 152) and sew to each point on row 1.

lace puff pattern

(multiple of 12 sts plus 2)

Row 1 (RS) K1, *ssk, k3, yo, p2, yo, k3, k2tog; rep from *, end k1.

Row 2 K1, *p2tog, p2, yo, k4, yo, p2, p2tog tbl; rep from *, end k1.

Row 3 K1, *ssk, k1, yo, p6, yo, k1, k2tog; rep from *, end k1.

Row 4 K1, *p2tog, yo, k8, yo, p2tog tbl; rep from *, end k1.

Row 5 K1, *p1, yo, k3, k2tog, ssk, k3, yo, p1; rep from *, end k1.

Row 6 K1, *k2, yo, p2, p2tog tbl, p2tog, p2, yo, k2; rep from *, end k1.

Row 7 K1, *p3, yo, k1, k2tog, ssk, k1, yo, p3; rep from *, end k1.

Row 8 K1, *k4, yo, p2tog tbl, p2tog, yo, k4; rep from *, end k1.

Rep rows 1–8.

arrow lace cuff

▲ Cast on 51 sts.

Knit 2 rows.

Work in arrow lace pattern for 2½"/6.5cm.

Cont in St st.

Sew pearl trim around cuff.

arrow lace pattern

(multiple of 10 sts plus 1)

Row 1 (RS) K1, *(yo, [sl 1, k1, psso]) twice, k1, [k2tog, yo] twice, k1; rep from * to end.

Row 2 Purl.

Row 3 K2, *yo, [sl 1, k1, psso], yo, [sl 1, k2tog, psso], yo, k2tog, yo, k3; rep from *, end yo, [sl 1, k1, psso], yo, [sl 1, k2tog, psso], yo, k2tog, k2.

Row 4 Purl.

Rep rows 1–4 for arrow lace.

beaded smocked collar/cuff

collar

▲ Cast on 106 sts.

Work in 2x2 smocked rib for 12 rows.

Cont in 1x1 rib for 4½"/10cm.

Bind off.

Fold rib to inside and sew bound-off edge to beg of rib.

Sew bead between each k2 rib on row 1.

cuff

▲ Cast on 66 sts.

Work in 2x2 smocked rib for 12 rows.

Cont in St st or 1x1 rib.

Sew bead between each k2 rib on row 1.

2x2 smocked rib

(multiple of 8 sts plus 10)

Rows 1, 3 and 5 (WS) *K2, p2; rep from *, end k2.

Rows 2 and 4 *P2, k2; rep from *, end p2.

Row 6 (RS) *P2, tie 6 sts [sl 6 sts on dpn and hold at front of work, wind the working yarn around the 6 sts twice, then k2, p2, k2 off the dpn]; rep from *, end p2, tie 6 sts, p2.

Rows 7, 9 and 11 *K2, p2; rep from *, end k2.

Rows 8 and 10 *P2, k2; rep from *, end k2.

Row 12 (RS) P2, k 2, p2, *tie 6 sts, p2; rep from *, end k2, p2.

Rep rows 1–12.

& collars

bold bell ruffle pattern

(beg with a multiple of 8 sts plus 7)

Row 1 (RS) P7, *k1, p7; rep from * to end.

Row 2 K7, *p1, k7; rep from * to end.

Row 3 P7, *yo, k1, yo, p7; rep from * to end.

Row 4 K7, *p2, p1 tbl, k7; rep from * to end.

Row 5 P7, *yo, k3, yo, p7; rep from * to end.

Row 6 K7, *p4, p1 tbl, k7; rep from * to end.

Row 7 P7, *yo, k5, yo, p7; rep from * to end.

Row 8 K7, *p6, p1 tbl, k7; rep from * to end.

Row 9 P7, *yo, k7, yo, p7; rep from * to end.

Row 10 K7, *p8, p1 tbl, k7; rep from * to end.

Row 11 P7, *yo, k9, yo, p7; rep from * to end.

Row 12 K7, *p10, p1 tbl, k7; rep from * to end.

Row 13 P7, *yo, k11, yo, p7; rep from * to end.

Row 14 K7, *p12, p1 tbl, k7, rep from * to end.

Rows 1 to 14 form bold bell ruffle.

bold bell ruffle collar

▼ Cast on 87 sts.

Work in 1x1 rib for 2"/5cm.

Work in bold bell ruffle pattern for 14 rows keeping
first st and last st in St st for selvedge sts.

Bind off.

Thread ribbon through row 1.

petite bell cuff with flowers

▲ Cast on 123 sts.

Work in petite bell pattern for desired length.

Cont in reverse St st.

Sew purchased flowers to every other point.

petite bell pattern

(beg with a multiple of 12 sts plus 3 to end with a multiple of 4
sts plus 3)

Row 1 (RS) P3, *k9, p3; rep from * to end.

Row 2 K3, *p9, k3; rep from * to end.

Row 3 P3, *skp, k5, k2tog, p3; rep from * to end.

Row 4 K3, *p7, k3; rep from * to end.

Row 5 P3, *skp, k3, k2tog, p3; rep from * to end.

Row 6 K3, *p5, k3; rep from * to end.

Row 7 P3, *skp, k1, k2tog, p3; rep from * to end.

Row 8 K3, *p3, k3; rep from * to end.

Row 9 P3, *SK2P, p3; rep from * to end.

Row 10 K3, *p1, k3; rep from * to end.

Row 11 P3, *k1, p3; rep from * to end.

Row 12 Rep row 10.

Cont to rep rows 11 and 12 for 1x3 rib.

smocked cuff

▲ Cast on 58 sts.

Work in smocked pattern for 18 rows.

Cont in St st.

smocked collar

▲ Cast on 106 sts.

Work in smocked pattern for 18 rows.

Bind off.

smocked pattern

(multiple of 8 sts plus 2)

Rows 1, 3 and 5 (WS) *K2, p2; rep from *, end k2.

Rows 2 and 4 *P2, k2; rep from *, end p2.

Row 6 *P2, tie 6 sts [sl 6 sts to dpn and hold to front of work, wind the working yarn around the 6 sts twice, then k2, p2, k2 from dpn];
rep from *, end p2, tie 6 sts, p2.

Rows 7, 9 and 11 *K2, p2; rep from *, end k2.

Rows 8 and 10 *P2, k2; rep from *, end k2.

Row 12 P2, tie 2, p2, *tie 6 sts, p2; rep from *, end tie 2, p2.

Rows 13–18 Rep rows 1–6.

Rep rows 1–18 once.

2x2 smocked rib

(multiple of 8 sts plus 2)

Rows 1, 3 and 5 (WS) *K2, p2; rep from *, end k2.

Rows 2 and 4 *P2, k2; rep from *, end p2.

Row 6 *P2, tie 6 sts [sl 6 sts to dpn and hold to front of work, wind the working yarn around the 6 sts twice, then k2, p2, k2 from dpn);

rep from *, end p2, tie 6 sts, p2.

Rows 7, 9 and 11 *K2, p2; rep from *, end k2.

Rows 8 and 10 *P2, k2; rep from *, end k2.

Row 12 P2, k2, p2, *tie 6 sts, p2; rep from *, end k2, p2.

2x2 smocked rib ruffle collar/cuff

collar

▲ Cast on 159 sts.

Knit 2 rows.

Work in St st for 2"/5cm, end WS row.

Next row *K1, k2tog; rep from * across—106 sts.

Purl next row.

Work in 2x2 smocked rib for 12 rows.

Bind off.

cuff

▲ Cast on 87 sts.

Knit 2 rows.

Work in St st for 2"/5cm, end WS row.

Next row *K1, k2tog; rep from * across—58 sts.

Purl next row.

Work in 2x2 smocked rib for 12 rows.

Cont in St st.

petite bell ruffle pattern

(beg with a multiple of 12 sts plus 3 to end with a multiple of 4 sts plus 3)

Row 1 (RS) P3, *k9, p3; rep from * to end.

Row 2 K3, *p9, k3; rep from * to end.

Row 3 P3, *SKP, k5, k2tog, p3; rep from * to end.

Row 4 K3, *p7, k3; rep from * to end.

Row 5 P3, *SKP, k3, k2tog, p3; rep from * to end.

Row 6 K3, *p5, k3; rep from * to end.

Row 7 P3, *SKP, k1, k2tog, p3; rep from * to end.

Row 8 K3, *p3, k3; rep from * to end.

Row 9 P3, *SK2P, p3; rep from * to end.

Row 10 K3, *p1, k3; rep from * to end.

Row 11 P3, *k1, p3; rep from * to end.

Row 12 Rep row 10.

Rep rows 11 and 12 for p3, k1 rib as desired.

triple petite bell ruffle cuff

▲ Cast on 123 sts.

Bottom layer Work rows 1 to 12 of petite bell ruffle pattern, then rep rows 11 and 12 for 3"/7.5cm. Place 43 sts on a spare needle.

Middle layer Work rows 1 to 12 of petite bell ruffle pattern, then rep rows 11 and 12 for 2"/5cm. Place 43 sts on a spare needle.

Top layer Work rows 1 to 12 of petite bell ruffle pattern, then rep rows 11 and 12 for 1"/2.5cm. Place 43 sts on a spare needle.

Join layers Work sts of all three layers tog, using 3-needle joining technique (see page 152).

spiral ruffle collar

Colors A and B

▼ With color A, cast on 88 sts.

Work in 1x1 rib for 4"/10cm.

Work in spiral ruffle pattern for 16 rows.

With color B (angora), knit 2 rows.

Fold rib to wrong side and sew cast-on edge to last row of rib.

Bind off.

spiral ruffle pattern

(beg with a multiple of 4 sts)

Row 1 (RS) *K4, yo; rep from *, end k4.

Row 2 and all WS rows Purl.

Row 3 *K5, yo; rep from *, end k4.

Row 4 Purl.

Row 5 *K6, yo; rep from *, end k4.

Row 7 *K7, yo; rep from *, end k4.

Row 9 *K8, yo; rep from *, end k4.

Cont inc as established, working one more st before each yo on every RS row until desired length, end with a WS row.

triple petite bell ruffle collar

▲ Cast on 255 sts.

Bottom layer Work rows 1 to 12 of petite bell ruffle, then rep rows 11 and 12 for 3"/7.5cm. Place 87 sts on a spare needle.

Middle layer Work rows 1 to 12 of petite bell ruffle, then rep rows 11 and 12 for 2"/5cm. Place 87 sts on a spare needle.

Top layer Work rows 1 to 12 of petite bell ruffle, then rep rows 11 and 12 for 1"/2.5cm. Place 87 sts on a spare needle.

Join layers Work sts of all three layers tog, using 3-needle joining technique (see page 154).

peplum ruffle pattern

(beg with a multiple of 5 sts plus 4)

Row 1 (RS) K3, *[inc 1 st in next st] twice, k3; rep from *, end last rep k4.

Row 2 and all WS rows Purl.

Row 3 K4, *[inc 1 st in next st] twice, k5; rep from *, end last rep k5.

Row 5 K5, *[inc 1 st in next st] twice, k7; rep from *, end last rep k6.

Row 7 K6, *[inc 1 st in next st] twice, k9; rep from *, end last rep k7.

Row 9 K7, *[inc 1 st in next st] twice, k11; rep from *, end last rep k8.

Cont inc as established, working 2 more sts after double inc on every RS row, end with a WS row.

peplum ruffle collar/cuff

collar

▼ Cast on 89 sts.

Work in k1, p1 rib for 4"/10cm.

Work in peplum ruffle pattern for 14 rows.

Bind off.

Fold rib to WS and sew cast-on edge to last row of rib.

Sew beads to bound-off edge.

cuff

▼ Begin with 44 sts.

Work in k1, p1 rib for 2½"/6.5cm.

Work in peplum ruffle pattern for 2½"/6.5cm.

Bind off.

Sew beads to bound-off edge.

& collars

spoke point ruffle collar/cuff

collar

▲ Cast on 179 sts.

First ruffle Work rows 1–10 of spoke point ruffle pattern. Cont in St st for 10 rows.
Place sts on a holder.

Second ruffle Work rows 1–10 of spoke point ruffle pattern.

Join ruffles Place 2nd ruffle over first ruffle and join using 3-needle joining technique (see page 152).
Work in 1x1 rib for 2"/5cm.
Bind off.

cuff

▲ Cast on 95 sts.

First ruffle Work rows 1–10 of spoke point ruffle pattern. Cont in St st for 10 rows.
Place sts on a holder.

Second ruffle Work rows 1–10 of spoke point ruffle pattern.

Joining ruffles Place 2nd ruffle over first ruffle and join using 3-needle joining technique (see page 152).
Cont in 1x1 rib.

spoke point ruffle pattern
(beg with a multiple of 14 sts plus 11)
Row 1 (RS) Knit.
Row 2 and all WS rows Purl.
Row 3 K11, *DD, k11; rep from * to end.

Row 5 K10, *DD, k9; rep from *, end last rep k10.
Row 7 K9, *DD, k7; rep from *, end last rep k9.
Row 9 K8, *DD, k5; rep from *, end last rep k8.
Row 10 Purl.
Rows 1–10 form spoke point ruffle.

cuffs

fluted edge collar/cuff

collar

▼ Cast on 98 sts.

Work in 1x1 rib for 3"/7.5cm.

Work rows 1–21 of fluted edge pattern.

Bind off.

Add purchased small ribbon flowers with pearl in center of each pat rep.

cuff

▼ Cast on 44.

Work in 1x1 rib for 3"/7.5cm.

Work rows 1–21 of fluted edge pattern.

Bind off.

Add purchased small ribbon flowers with pearl in center of each pat rep.

fluted edge pattern

(beg with a multiple of 6 sts plus 2)

Rows 1, 3 and 5 P2, *k4, p2; rep from * to end.

Rows 2, 4 and 6 K2, *p4, k2; rep from * to end.

Row 7 P2, *k2, yo, k2, p2; rep from * to end.

Row 8 K2, *p5, k2; rep from * to end.

Row 9 P2, *k2, yo, k1, yo, k2, p2; rep from * to end.

Row 10 K2, *p7, k2; rep from * to end.

Row 11 P2, *k2, yo, k3, yo, k2, p2; rep from * to end.

Row 12 K2, *p9, k2; rep from * to end.

Row 13 P2, *k2, yo, k5, yo, k2, p2; rep from * to end.

Row 14 K2, *p11, k2; rep from * to end.

Row 15 P2, *k2, yo, k7, yo, k2, p2; rep from * to end.

Row 16 K2, *p13, k2; rep from * to end.

Row 17 P2, *k2, yo, k9, yo, k2, p2; rep from * to end.

Row 18 K2, *p15, k2; rep from * to end.

Row 19 P2, *k2, yo, k11, yo, k2, p2; rep from * to end.

Row 20 K2, *p17, k2; rep from * to end.

Row 21 P2, *k2, yo, k13, yo, k2, p2; rep from * to end.

Rows 1 to 21 form fluted edge.

& collars

1x1 rib cuff with i-cord

▲ Cast on 44 sts.

Work in 1x1 rib pattern for 3"/7.5cm.

Cont in St st.

Make 5-st I-Cord (see page 154) to fit around cuff along last row of rib.

Sew purchased 1"/2.5cm and 2"/5cm long bead tassels alternately to every other st of rib.

Sew I-Cord to last row of rib (see page 154).

1x1 rib pattern

(multiple of 2 sts)

Row 1 *K1, p1; rep from * across.

Rep row 1.

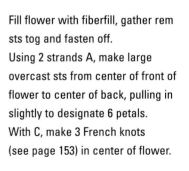

1x1 rib cuff with ruffle flower

▲ Cast on 40 sts.

Work in 1x1 rib pattern for 5"/12.5cm.

Cont in St st.

Fold cuff in half to right side of sleeve.

Make ruffle flower and sew to cuff.

ruffle flower pattern

Colors A, B and C

With A, cast on 13 sts, leaving a long tail for seaming.

Row 1 (RS) Knit.

Rows 2, 4 and 6 Purl.

Row 3 K1, *k1, M1, k1; rep from * to end.

Row 5 K1, *k2, M1, k1; rep from * to end.

Row 7 K1, *k3, M1, k1; rep from * to end.

Row 8 Purl. Change to B.

Row 9 Knit.

Rows 10, 12, 14 and 16 Purl.

Row 11 K1, *k2, k2tog, k1; rep from * to end.

Row 13 K1, *k1, k2tog, k1; rep from * to end.

Row 15 K1, *k2tog, k1; rep from * to end.

Fill flower with fiberfill, gather rem sts tog and fasten off.

Using 2 strands A, make large overcast sts from center of front of flower to center of back, pulling in slightly to designate 6 petals.

With C, make 3 French knots (see page 153) in center of flower.

2x2 rib cuff

▲ Cast on 40 sts.

Work in 2x2 rib pattern for 2"/5cm.

Cont in St st.

Fold cuff in half to wrong side of sleeve and sew in place placing fiberfill inside.

2x2 rib pattern

(multiple of 4 sts)

Row 1 *K2, p2; rep from * across.

Rep row 1 for 2x2 rib.

medallion rib cuff

Colors A and B

▲ With A, cast on 44 sts.

Knit 2 rows.

Work in medallion rib pattern for 2½"/6.5cm.

Cont in St st.

With B (angora), work whip sts along lower edge of cuff.

medallion rib pattern

(multiple of 8 sts plus 4)

Row 1 (RS) P4, *sl 2 wyib, [knit the 2nd st on LH needle, then the first st slipping both sts from needle tog], p4; rep from * to end.

Row 2 K4, *sl 2 wyif, [purl the 2nd st on LH needle, then the first st slipping both sts from needle tog], k4; rep from * to end.

Row 3 Knit.

Row 4 Purl.

Rep rows 1–4.

& collars

diagonal eyelet ruffle collar

▲ Cast on 84 sts.

Work in diagonal eyelet ruffle pattern for 16 rows.

Work in St st for 1"/2.5cm.

Purl next RS row for turning ridge.

Purl next row.

Cont in St st for 1"/2.5cm.

Bind off. Fold along turning ridge and sew hem to WS.

Sew sequins evenly spaced on collar.

diagonal eyelet ruffle pattern

(multiple of 7 sts)

Preparation row K1, *p5, k2; rep from *, end last rep k1.

Row 1 (RS) P1, *yo, k2tog, k3, p2; rep from *, end last rep p1.

Rows 2, 4 and 6 K1, *p5, k2; rep from *, end last rep k1.

Row 3 P1, *k1, yo, k2tog, k2, p2; rep from *, end last rep p1.

Row 5 P1, *k2, yo, k2tog, k1, p2; rep from *, end last rep p1.

Row 7 P1, *k3, yo, k2tog, p2; rep from *, end last rep p1.

Row 8 Rep row 2.

Rep rows 1–8.

block arrowhead ruffle collar

▲ Cast on 91 sts.

Work in block arrowhead ruffle pattern for 24 rows.

Work in St st for 1½"/3.8cm.

Bind off. Collar edge will roll to RS.

Sew 2 rows of purchased flower appliqués evenly spaced.

block arrowhead ruffle pattern

(multiple of 13 sts)

Rows 1 and 3 (WS) K2, *p4, k1, p4, k4; rep from *, end last rep k2.

Row 2 P2, *yo, SKP, k2, p1, k2, k2tog, yo, p4; rep from *, end last rep p2.

Row 4 P2, *k1, yo, SKP, k1, p1, k1, k2tog, yo, k1, p4; rep from *, end last rep p2.

Rows 5 and 7 P6, *k1, p12; rep from *, end last rep p6.

Row 6 K4, *yo, SKP, p1, k2tog, yo, k8; rep from *, end last rep k4.

Row 8 K5, *yo, SK2P, yo, k10; rep from *, end last rep k5.

Rep rows 1–8.

cleo collar

▲ Cast on 177 sts.

Knit 2 rows.

Work in 1x3 rib pattern for 3"/7.5cm.

Next row (RS) K1, *p3tog, k1; rep from * to end.

Work in seed st for 3 rows.

Bind off.

Make a 3-st I-Cord (see page 152) long enough to reach around collar before decrease row.

Sew a purchased 2½"/6.5cm length of beads between each k1 rib on last row of rib.

Sew I-Cord along decrease row.

1x3 rib pattern

(multiple of 4 sts plus 1)

Row 1 (RS) K1 *p3, k1; rep from * to end.

Row 2 P1, *k3, p1; rep from * to end.

Rep rows 1–2.

double rolled edge collar

▲ Cast on 82 sts.

Work in St st for 3"/7.5cm. Bind off.

Cast-on and bound-off edges will roll together naturally.

Sew to neck edge along center of collar.

bubble cuff

▲ Cast on 43 sts.

Work in bubble pattern for 24 rows.

Cont in St st.

Sew beads between bubbles.

bubble pattern

(multiple of 4 plus 3)

K5B (Knit the 5th st below): Sl the next st off LH needle and drop 4 rows down. Insert point of RH needle under strands and into the st on the 5th row down, insert LH needle under the strands and into the st. Knit the st normally catching the strands at the same time.

Preparation row (WS) Purl.

Rows 1–4 Work in St st, starting with a k row.

Row 5 K3, *K5B, k3; rep from * to end.

Row 6 Purl.

Rows 7–10 Work in St st, starting with k row.

Row 11 K1, *K5B, k3; rep from * to last 2 sts, K5B, k1.

Row 12 Purl.

Rep rows 1–12.

brick border cuff

▲ With A, cast on 45 sts.

Knit 2 rows.

Work in brick border pattern for 24 rows.

With A, cont in St st.

brick border pattern

(multiple of 6 sts plus 3)

Colors A and B

Preparation rows Knit 2 rows.

Row 1 (RS) Using A, knit.

Row 2 Using A, purl.

Row 3 Using B, k4, sl 1, *k5, sl 1; rep from *, end k4.

Row 4 Using B, k4, sl 1 wyif, *k5, sl 1 wyif; rep from *, end k4.

Row 5 Using B, p4, sl 1 wyib, *p5, sl 1 wyib; rep from *, end p4.

Row 6 Rep row 4.

Row 7 Using A, knit.

Row 8 Using, A, purl.

Row 9 Using B, k1, sl 1, *k5, sl 1; rep

from *, end k1.

Row 10 Using B, k1, sl 1 wyif, *k5, sl 1 wyif; rep from *, end k1.

Row 11 Using B, p1, sl 1 wyib, *p5, sl 1 wyib; rep from *, end p1.

Row 12 Rep row 10.

Rep rows 1–12.

happy honeycomb cuffs

Version 1

Version 2

▲ With A, cast on 44 sts.

Work in happy honeycomb pattern for 32 rows.

With B, cont in St st.

Version 1

Version 2

▲ With A, cast on 60 sts.

Work in happy honeycomb pattern for 32 rows.

With B, cont in St st, dec 16 sts evenly spaced on first row.

happy honeycomb pattern

(multiple of 8 plus 4)

Colors A, B and C

Row 1 (RS) Using A, knit.

Row 2 Using A, purl.

Row 3 Using B, k1, sl 2, *k6, sl 2; rep from *, end k1.

Row 4 Using B, p1, sl 2, *p6, sl 2; rep from *, end p1.

Rows 5–8 Rep the last 2 rows twice more.

Row 9 Using A, knit.

Row 10 Using A, purl.

Row 11 Using C, k5, sl 2, *k6, sl 2; rep from *, end k5.

Row 12 Using C, p5, sl 2, *p6, sl 2; rep from *, end p5.

Rows 13–16 Rep last 2 rows twice more.

Rep rows 1–16.

i-cord scroll collar/cuff

collar

▲ Cast on 80 sts.

Work in St st for 5"/12.5cm, end with WS row.

Purl next row on RS for turning ridge.

Purl next row.

Work in St st for 1"/2.5cm.

Bind off. Sew bound-off edge to cast-on edge.

Make a long 3-st I-Cord and place sts on a holder.

Follow diagram to shape cord and adjust for length. Fasten off and sew cord (see page 154) in position on collar.

cuff

▲ Cast on 40 sts.

Work in St st for 5"/12.5cm.

Place sts on a holder.

Make a long 3-st I-Cord and place sts on a holder.

Follow diagram to shape cord and adjust for length. Fasten off and sew cord (see page 154) in position on cuff.

stockinette st i-cord

(When making I-Cord, use two double-pointed needles or one short circular needle.)

▶ Cast on desired number of sts.

Row 1 Knit, do not turn, slide sts to other end of needle.

Rep row 1 for desired length.

Bind off.

• start
• end

point cuff with picot

▲ Cast on 53 sts.

Row 1 Knit.

Row 2 Purl.

Row 3 K2, *yo, k2tog; rep from *, end k1.

Row 4 Purl

Row 5 K24, k2tog, k1, k2tog, k24.

Rows 6, 8, 10, 12 and 14 Purl.

Row 7 K23, k2tog, k1, k2tog, k23.

Row 9 K22, k2tog, k1, k2tog, k22.

Row 11 K21, k2tog, k1, k2tog, k21.

Row 13 K20, k2tog, k1, k2tog, k 20.

Cont in St st.

Fold hem to WS at row 3 to form picot edge and sew in place.

Sew appliqué to cuff.

point cuff with cable

▲ Cast on 43 sts.

Row 1 (RS) K19, SKP, k1, k2tog, k19.

Row 2 and all WS rows Purl.

Row 3 K18, SKP, k1, k2tog, k18.

Row 5 K17, SKP, k1, k2tog, k17.

Cont to rep dec row every RS row working 1 st less on each side of center st until 29 sts remain, end WS row.

Next row (RS) Knit across dec 1 st in center—28 sts.

Purl next row.

Begin cable pat

Row 1 (RS) K10, row 1 of cable on next 8 sts, k10.

Row 2 P10, row 2 of cable on next 8 sts, p10.

Cont cable pat on center 8 sts and St st on each side of these 8 sts.

cable pattern

(worked on 8 sts)

Row 1 (RS) P1, sl 3 sts to cn and hold in front, k3, k3 from cn, p1.

Rows 2, 4, 6 and 8 K1, p6, k1.

Row 3, 5 and 7 P1, k6, p1.

Rep rows 1–8 for cable.

& collars

deep point cuff with fur and flowers

▲ Cast on 1 st.

Row 1 (RS) K in front, back and front of st—3 sts.

Row 2 Purl.

Work in St st, inc 1 st in first and last st every RS row 4 times—11 sts.

Cont in St st and cast on 2 sts at end of next 16 rows—43 sts.

Cont in St st.

Sew fur trim to point.

Sew four decorative buttons up center of cuff.

cable rib ruffle cuff

▼ Working on a multiple of 4 sts plus 2, work in baby cable rib pattern for 3"/7.5cm.

ruffle

Row 1 (RS) *P2, [k in front, back and front] of next 2 sts—6 sts; rep from *, end p2.

Row 2 (WS) *K2, p6; rep from *, end k2.

Row 3 *P2, k6; rep from *, end p2.

Row 4 Rep row 2.

Rep rows 3 and 4 for 1"/2.4cm.

Bind off.

baby cable rib pattern

(multiple of 4 sts plus 2)

RT Skip first st on LH needle and knit the 2nd st. Then knit the first st and slip both off of LH needle.

Row 1 (RS) *P2, k2; rep from *, end p2.

Row 2 K2, *p2, k2; rep from * to end.

Row 3 *P2, RT; rep from *, end p2.

Row 4 Rep row 2.

Rep rows 1–4.

lace ladder/twist cuff

▲ Cast on 48 sts.

Knit 2 rows.

Work in lace ladder/twist pattern for 2½"/6.5cm.

Cont in St st.

lace ladder/twist pattern

(multiple of 7 sts plus 6)

Row 1 (RS) K1, *k2tog, [yo] twice, ssk, k3; rep from *, end last rep k1.

Row 2 K1, *k 1, [k1 tbl, k1] into double yo of previous row, k1, p3; rep from *, end k1, [k1 tbl, k1] into double yo, k2.

Row 3 K1 *k2tog, [yo] twice, ssk, skip next 2 sts and k into 3rd st, then k into 2nd st, then k into first, then sl all 3 sts from needle together; rep from *, end k2tog, [yo] twice, ssk, k1.

Row 4 Rep row 2.

Rep rows 1–4.

poet cuff

Note 2 needle sizes are used, one needle 3 sizes larger than the other.

Colors A and B

▲ With larger needles and A (mohair), cast on 88 sts.

Work in St st for 2"/5cm.

*Change to smaller needles and B.

Next row (RS) K2tog to end.

K 3 rows.* Change to larger needles and A.

Next row K in front and back of each st.

Work in St st for 7"/18cm.

Rep from * to * once.

Cont as desired.

Thread narrow silk ribbon through first ruching section.

eyelet towers cuff

▲ Cast on 41 sts.

Work in St st for 3 rows.

Knit 1 row on WS.

Work in eyelet towers pattern for 16 rows.

Cont in St st.

Lace ribbon through eyelets on rows 1 and 9.

eyelet towers pattern

(multiple of 4 sts plus 1)

Row 1 (RS) P4, *k1, p1, yo, p2tog; rep from *, end p1.

Row 2 K4, *p1, k3; rep from *, end k1.

Row 3 P4, *k1, p3; rep from *, end p1.

Rows 4–7 Rep rows 2 and 3 twice more.

Row 8 Knit.

Row 9 P2, *k1, p1, yo, p2tog; rep from *, end k1, p2.

Row 10 K2, *p1, k3; rep from *, end p1, k2.

Row 11 P2, *k1, p3; rep from *, end k1, p2.

Rows 12–15 Rep rows 10 and 11 twice more.

Row 16 Knit.

Rep rows 1–16.

eiffel tower cuff

▲ Cast on 41 sts.

Work in St st for 3 rows.

Knit 1 row on WS.

Work eiffel pattern for 16 rows.

Cont in St st.

eiffel pattern

(multiple of 4 sts plus 1)

Row 1 (RS) P4, *yo, p2tog, p2; rep from *, end p1.

Row 2 K4, *p1, k3; rep from *, end k1.

Row 3 P4, *k1, p3; rep from *, end p1.

Rows 4–7 Rep rows 2 and 3 twice more.

Row 8 Knit.

Row 9 P2, *yo, p2tog, p2; rep from *, end last rep p1.

Row 10 K2, *p1, k3; rep from *, end last rep k2.

Row 11 P2, *k1, p3; rep from *, end last rep p2.

Rows 12–15 Rep rows 10 and 11 twice more.

Row 16 Knit.

Rep rows 1–16.

princess cuff

Note 2 needle sizes are used, one needle 2 sizes larger than the other.

Colors A and B

▲ With smaller needles and B, cast on 38 sts.

Knit 12 rows. Change to larger needles and A (mohair).

Next row (RS) K in front and back of each st—76 sts.

Work in St st for 2½"/6.5cm.

*Change to smaller needles and B.

Next row (RS) K2tog across.

Knit 5 rows.* Change to larger needles and A.

Next row K in front and back of each st

Work in St st for 2½"/6.5cm.

Rep from * to * once.

Cont in St st.

& collars

keyhole cuff

Colors A and B

▲ With straight needles and A, cast on 44 sts.

Work in garter st for 6 rows.

Work 2 rows in St st.

Dec 1 st each side every other row 5 times.

Work 2 rows even.

Inc 1 st each side every other row 5 times.

Using 4 dpns, join and work around in St st (k every rnd),

inc 1 st on first row at point.

Cont in St st.

Using B (angora), make a 3-st I-Cord (see page 152) and sew around keyhole.

Using A, make a buttonloop at bottom of cuff and sew button opposite buttonloop.

point cuff with rib

▼ Beg with 45 sts. Work in St st for 2 rows. Work short rows as foll: K30, work wrap & turn (w&t) as foll: sl 1, bring yarn to front, sl same st back to LH needle, turn work; p15, work w&t as foll: sl 1, bring yarn to back of work, sl same st back to LH needle, turn work; k13, w&t as before; p11, w&t as before; cont in this way to work 2 less sts at end of every row until last row worked is k1. Turn work and purl to end of row, working the wrap at every short row tog with corresponding st on needle. Turn and k all 45 sts, working the wrap at every short row tog with corresponding st on needle. Work in 1x1 rib over all sts for 1". Bind off in rib.

Version 2

corkscrew and seed stitch collar/cuff

collar

▲ Cast on 66 sts.

Work corkscrew pattern, leaving last stitch after binding off on RH needle.

Pick up sts on corkscrews—*Cast on 3 sts to RH needle, skip next 8 sts, twist corkscrew, pick up next st on bound-off edge; rep from *, end pick up last st of corkscrew—89 sts.

Work in seed st for 2"/5cm, end with a WS row.

Leave on a spare needle.

Work another corkscrew edge and 2 rows seed st.

Place 2nd corkscrew over first corkscrew and join using 3-needle joining technique (see page 152) in pat.

Cont in seed st for 1½"/3.6cm.

Knit 1 row on WS for turning ridge.

Cont in St st for 1½"/3.6cm.

Bind off.

Version 1

Fold St st hem to WS and sew in place.

Version 2

Allow St st to roll, cross left end over right.

cuff

Cast on 30 sts and work same as for Collar on 41 sts.

Version 1

corkscrew pattern

(Cast on over two needles or very loosely the given number of sts.)

Row 1 K in front, back and front of each st across.

Row 2 Bind off purlwise.

Use fingers to twist into a corkscrew.

rosey's ruffle collar/cuff

collar

▶ Cast on desired number of sts to fit V-neck opening.

Work rosey's ruffle pattern rows 1–13.

Bind off.

Sew ruffle to V-neck opening.

Deep V-neck Sleeveless sweater (shown) instructions on page 147.

cuff

▶ Cast on sts until piece measures 24"/61cm.

Work rosey's ruffle pattern rows 1–13.

Bind off.

Sew ruffle in a spiral around sleeve edge.

rosey's ruffle pattern

Cast on desired number of sts.

Row 1 Knit.

Row 2 Knit into front and back of each st.

Rows 3–9 Knit.

Row 10 Knit into front and back of each st.

Row 11 Knit.

Row 12 Knit into front and back of each st.

Row 13 Knit.

Bind off.

necklines

bold baroque cable and cord collar

▶ Cast on 54 sts.

Knit 1 row.

Work in bold baroque cable pattern keeping first 6 and last 6 sts in 2x2 rib as follows:

All RS rows K2, p2, k2, work bold baroque cable across center 42 sts, k2, p2, k2.

All WS rows P2, k2, p2, work bold baroque cable across center 42 sts, p2, k2, p2.

Work until piece measures 10"/25.5cm from beg.

Bind off 50 sts and fasten off 51st st. Unravel last 3 sts and steam fringe lightly.

Knot each fringe loop at edge.

Work two I-Cords (see page 154) each 9"/22.5cm long. Sew to each upper collar edge.

6-st LC Sl 3 sts to cn and hold in front, k3, then k3 from cn.

6-st RC Sl 3 sts to cn and hold in back, k3, then k3 from cn.

4-st LPC Sl 3 sts to cn and hold in front, p1, then k3 from cn.

4-st RPC Sl 1 st to cn and hold in back, k3, then p1 from cn.

5-st LPC Sl 3 sts to cn and hold in front, p2, then k3 from cn.

5-st RPC Sl 2 sts to cn and hold in back, k3, then p2 from cn.

6-st LPC Sl 3 sts to cn and hold in front, p3, then k3 from cn.

6-st RPC Sl 3 sts to cn and hold in back, k3, then p3 from cn.

double zigzag rib collar

▶ Cast on 26 sts.

Knit 1 row.

Work first 3 and last 3 sts in reverse St st and center 20 sts in double zigzag pattern until desired length.

Bind off 22 sts and fasten off 23rd st.

Unravel last 3 sts and steam lightly.

Pick up sts evenly across opposite edge and work in St st for 1"/2.5cm. Fold to WS and sew in place.

Add pearls or beads to center of each motif.

double zigzag pattern

(panel of 20 sts)

3-st RPC Sl 1 st to cn and hold in back, k2, then p1 from cn.

3-st LPC Sl 2 sts to cn and hold in front, p1, then k2 from cn.

Row 1 (WS) K3, p2, k3, p4, k3, p2, k3.

Row 2 [P2, 3-st RPC] twice, [3-st LPC, p2] twice.

Row 3 and all WS rows K the knit sts and p the purl sts.

Row 4 P1, [3-st RPC, p2] twice, 3-st LPC, p2, 3-st LPC, p1.

Row 6 [3-st RPC, p2] twice, [p2, 3-st LPC] twice.

Row 8 [3-st LPC, p2] twice, [p2, 3-st RPC] twice.

Row 10 P1, [3-st LPC, p2] twice, 3-st RPC, p2, 3-st RPC, p1.

Row 12 [P2, 3-st LPC] twice, [3-st RPC, p2] twice.

Rep rows 1–12.

bold baroque cable pattern

(over 42 sts)

Rows 1 and 3 (WS) K3, p3, k2, p3, k7, p6, k7, p3, k2, p3, k3.

Row 2 P3, k3, p2, k3, p7, k6, p7, k3, p2, k3, p3.

Row 4 P3, 4-st LPC, 4-st RPC, p7, 6-st LPC, p7, 4-st LPC, 4-st RPC, p3.

Row 5 and all WS rows Knit the knit sts and purl the purl sts.

Row 6 P4, 6-st LC, p6, 5-st RPC, 5-st LPC, p6, 6-st LC, p4.

Row 8 P4, k3, 4-st LPC, p3, 5-st RPC, p4, 5-st LPC, p3, 4-st RPC, k3, p4.

Row 10 P4, [4-st LPC] twice, 5-st RPC, p8, 5-st LPC, [4-st RPC] twice, p4.

Row 12 P5, 4-st LPC, 6-st RC, p12, 6-st LC, 4-st RPC, p5.

Row 14 P6, 6-st LC, 6-st LPC, p6, 6-st RPC, 6-st RC, p6.

Row 16 P5, 4-st RPC, [6-st LPC] twice, [6-st RPC] twice, 4-st LPC, p5.

Row 18 P4, 4-st RPC, p4, 6-st LPC, 6-st LC, 6-st RPC, p4, 4-st LPC, p4.

Row 20 P3, 4-st RPC, p8, [6-st RC] twice, p8, 4-st LPC, p3.

Row 22 P3, k3, p9, k3, 6-st LPC, k3, p9, k3, p3.

Row 24 P3, 4-st LPC, p8, [6-st RC] twice, p8, 4-st RPC, p3.

Row 26 P4, 4-st LPC, p4, 6-st RPC, 6-st LC, 6-st LPC, p4, 4-st RPC, p4.

Row 28 P5, 4-st LPC, [6-st RPC] twice, [6-st LPC] twice, 4-st RPC, p5.

Row 30 P6, 6-st LC, 6-st RPC, p6, 6-st LPC, 6-st RC, p6.

Row 32 P5, 4-st RPC, 6-st RC, p12, 6-st RC, 4-st LPC, p5.

Row 34 P4, [4-st RPC] twice, 5-st LPC, p8, 5-st RPC, [4-st LPC] twice, p4.

Row 36 P4, k3, 4-st RPC, p3, 5-st LPC, p4, 5-st RPC, p3, 4-st LPC, k3, p4.

Row 38 P4, 6-st LC, p6, 5-st LPC, 5-st RPC, p6, 6-st LC, p4.

Row 40 P3, 4-st RPC, 4-st LPC, p7, 6-st LC, p7, 4-st RPC, 4-st LPC, p3.

Row 42 Rep row 2.

Rep rows 1–42.

fancy bobble cable and fringe collar

▶ Cast on 22 sts.

Knit 1 row.

Work first 3 and last 3 sts in reverse St st and center 16 sts in fancy bobble cable pattern until desired length. Bind off 18 sts and fasten off 19th st. Unravel last 3 sts. Knot each fringe loop next to fabric; trim fringe to 1".

fancy bobble cable pattern

(panel of 16 sts)

MB (Make Bobble) [K1, p1, k1] in each of the next 2 sts, turn and p6, turn and k1, ssk, k2tog, k1, turn and [p2tog] twice, turn and k2.

4-st LC Sl 2 sts to cn and hold in front, k2, then k2 from cn.

4-st RC Sl 2 sts to cn and hold in back, k, then k2 from cn.

4-st LPC Sl 2 sts to cn and hold in front, p2, then k2 from cn.

4-st RPC Sl 2 sts to cn and hold in back, k2, then p2 from cn.

Row 1 (RS) P2, k4, p4, k4, p2.

Row 2 and all WS rows K the knit sts and p the purl sts.

Row 3 P2, 4-st LC, p4, 4-st RC, p2.

Row 5 P2, k4, p1, MB, p1, k4, p2.

Row 7 Rep row 3.

Row 9 Rep row 1.

Row 11 [4-st RPC, 4-st LPC] twice.

Row 13 K2, p4, k4, p4, k2.

Row 15 [4-st LPC, 4-st RPC] twice.

Row 16 K the knit sts and p the purl sts.

Rep rows 1–16.

enclosed cable and bead edge collar

▶ Cast on 32 sts.

Work first 4 and last 4 sts in 1x1 rib and center 24 sts in enclosed cable pattern until piece measures desired length. Bind off. Attach purchased beaded fringe to one long edge.

enclosed cable pattern

(panel of 24 sts)

6-st LC Sl 3 sts to cn and hold in front, k3, then k3 from cn.

6-st RC Sl 3 sts to cn and hold in back, k3, then k3 from cn.

5-st LPC Sl 3 sts to cn and hold in front, p2, then k3 from cn.

5-st RPC Sl 2 sts to cn and hold in back, k3, then p2 from cn.

Row 1 (RS) P2, k3, p4, k6, p4, k3, p2.

Row 2 and all WS rows K the knit sts and p the purl sts.

Row 3 P2, k3, p4, 6-st LC, p4, k3, p2.

Row 5 P2, k3, p4 k6, p4, k3, p2.

Row 7 P2, 5-st LPC, p2, k6, p2, 5-st RPC, p2.

Row 9 P4, 5-st LPC, 6-st LC, 5-st RPC, p4.

Row 11 P6, [6-st RC] twice, p6.

Row 13 P4, 5-st RPC, 6-st LC, 5-st LPC, p4.

Row 15 P2, 5-st RPC, p2, k6, p2, 5-st LPC, p2.

Row 16 K the knit sts and p the purl sts.

Rep rows 1–16.

wrap cross/bobble cord

▲ Cast on 5 sts.

Rows 1–5 Knit, do not turn, slide sts to other end of needle.

Row 6 K2, MB, k2, do not turn, slide sts to other end of needle.

Rep rows 1–6 to desired length. Bind off. Attach to neck edge.

Make bobble (MB) (K in front, back, front, back and front of st)—5 sts; turn, p5, pass 2nd, 3rd, 4th and 5th sts one at a time over first st.

6-st cable/cross cable

▲ Cast on 16 sts.

6-st LC Sl 3 sts to cn and hold in front, k3, then k3 from cn.

Row 1 and all WS rows P3, k2, p6, k2, p3.

Row 2 K3, p2, k6, p2, k3.

Row 4 K3, p2, 6-st LC, p2, k3.

Row 6 Rep row 2.

Rep rows 1–6 to desired length. Bind off. Attach to neck edge.

drop stitch scoop

▼ Pick up a multiple of 6 sts plus 5 sts around neck.

Work in St st for 4"/10cm.

Next row *Bind off 5 sts, drop 1 st; rep from *, end bind off 5 sts.

picot bind-off scoop

▼ (over even number of sts)

Note This edging is worked on last row of a piece.

Last row (RS) Bind off 2 sts, *sl st back to LH needle, using cable cast-on method (see page 152), cast on 3 sts, bind off 5 sts; rep from * to end. Fasten off.

eyelet double ruffle with ribbon

▲▶ Cast on an even number of sts.

Work in St st for 1"/2.5cm.

Eyelet row (RS) K1, *yo, k2tog; rep from *, end k1.

Cont in St st for 1"/2.5cm.

Bind off.

Run ribbon through eyelet row using large tapestry needle.

Sew to neck edge.

ruching turtleneck

▶ **Colors** A and B

Note 2 needle sizes are used, one needle 3 sizes larger than the other.

With smaller needles and A, cast on 15 sts.

*Knit 6 rows.

Change to larger needles and B.

Next row (RS) Knit in front and back of each st.

Work in St st for 9 rows.

Change to smaller needles and A.

Next row (RS) K2tog across.*

Rep from * to * 6 times more.

Knit 13 rows.

Bind off.

If desired, work 3 buttonholes evenly spaced across cast-on edge and sew 3 buttons on bound-off edge opposite buttons.

double picot eyelet

▲ ▶ Cast on an uneven number of sts.

Rows 1, 3 and 5 (WS) Purl.

Row 2 and 4 Knit.

Row 6 (picot row) K1, *yo, k2tog; rep from * to end.

Rep rows 1–6 twice more.

Then rep rows 1–5.

Bind off.

Fold outer eyelets to form picot.

Sew cast-on edge to bound-off edge at back center.

Run ribbon through center eyelet row.

Sew to neck edge at seam.

classic cable turtleneck

▲ Cast on 120 sts.

Work in classic cable turtleneck pattern for 16 rows or until desired length.

Bind off.

classic cable turtleneck pattern

(multiple of 8 sts)

4-st LC Sl next 2 sts to cn and hold in front, k2, then k2 from cn.

Rows 1 and 3 (WS) *K2, p4, k2; rep from * to end.

Row 2 *P2, k4, p2; rep from * to end.

Row 4 *P2, 4-st LC, p2; rep from * to end.

Rep rows 1–4.

seed stitch v-neck/button flower

▲ Cast on an uneven number of sts.

Row 1 K1, [p1, k1] to end.

Rep row 1 for 1"/2.5cm.

Bind off.

Sew to V-neck edge overlapping the left end over the right end. Sewing a purchased flower at the V.

boat neck/bobbles

▲ Cast on 63 sts.

Row 1 (RS) K15, k1, [p1, k1] across 32 sts, k15.

Row 2 P15, work in established rib across 33 sts, p15.

Rep rows 1 and 2 for 1"/2.5cm.

Bind off.

Make 8 bobbles and sew evenly across rib section.

MB (make bobble)

Cast on 1 st.

[K into front, back, front, back and front of st]—5 sts; turn, p5, pass 2nd, 3rd, 4th and 5th sts one at a time over first st.

i-cord ruffle v-neck

▶ **5-st I-Cord** With dpn, cast on 5 sts. *K5, do not turn, slide sts to other end of needle; rep from * until cord measures desired length.

Sew purchased ruffle to cord.

Sew cord to V-neck edge with a button at the V.

2x2 rib placket/cord tie and eyelet

▲ ▶ **Colors** A and B

First placket With RS facing and A, pick up 30 sts (or a multiple of 8 sts plus 6 sts) along pullover front neck opening.

Rows 1 and 3 (WS) P2, *k2, p2; rep from * to end.

Row 2 K2, *p2, k2; rep from * to end.

Row 4 (eyelet row) K2, *p2tog, yo, k2, p2, k2; rep from * twice more, p2tog, yo, k2.

Rows 5 and 7 Rep row 1.

Row 6 Rep row 2.

Row 8 Bind off in rib.

Second placket Work same as first placket along other side of front neck opening.

Sew edge of plackets to front neck bound-off sts.

Cord tie Using B, work a 3-st I-Cord (see page 154) approximately 30"/76cm or until desired length.

Bind off. Thread cord through eyelets.

1x1 rib neck t-twist

▲ Cast on 80 sts (or a multiple of 8 sts).

Work in 1x1 rib for 6 rows.

Next row (RS) *K8, then rotate LH needle counter-clockwise 360 degrees; rep from * to end.

Cont in 1x1 rib until desired length.

Bind off.

Sew to neck edge.

1x1 rib placket/collar/flowers/buttons

▲ **Colors** A and B

First placket With A, pick up an even number of sts along placket opening.

Work in 1x1 rib for 6 rows with A, then 2 rows with B. Bind off.

Second placket Work same as first placket along other side of front neck opening. Sew edge of plackets across front neck bound-off sts.

collar

With A, pick up an even number of sts along neck edge. Work in 1x1 rib for 4"/10cm with A, then 2 rows with B.

flowers

With B, cast on 4 sts, bind off 4 sts. *Sl rem st back onto LH needle, do not turn, cast on 3 sts, bind off 4 sts; rep from * 6 times more. Fasten off.

Run threaded tapestry needle through straight edge of piece.

Pull tightly and secure. Make desired number of flowers and sew to placket with button or pearl in center. Sew half of snap fastener to WS of right placket behind flower. Sew other half to RS of left placket corresponding to first half.

baby cable placket/collar

baby cable pattern

(multiple of 4 sts plus 2)

RT K2tog, but leave on needle; then insert RH needle between the 2 sts just knitted tog, and knit the first st again; then sl both sts from needle tog.

Rows 1 and 3 (WS) K2, *p2, k2; rep from * to end.

Row 2 P2, *k2, p2; rep from * to end.

Row 4 P2, *RT, p2; rep from * to end.

Rep rows 1–4.

collar

▲ With RS facing, pick up a multiple of 4 sts plus 2 sts plus 1 selvage st at each end.

Keeping 1 selvage st at each end in reverse St st, work in baby cable pattern for 5"/12.5cm, end with pat Row 1.

Bind off on pat Row 2.

button placket

▲ ▶ With RS facing, pick up a multiple of 4 sts plus 2 sts plus 1 selvage st at each end.

Keeping 1 selvage st at each end in reverse St st, work 12 rows of baby cable pattern, end with pat Row 1.

Bind off on pat Row 2.

buttonhole placket

▲ ▶ Work as for button placket, working 2-st buttonholes evenly spaced on 6th row.

Sew on buttons.

cowl collar/i-cord bolo

▲ Pick up desired amount of sts around neck edge. Work in St st for 5"/12.5cm.

Bind off. Collar will roll with WS showing.

cords

Make two 5-st I-Cords (see page 154) 24"/60cm in length and knot at each end.

Make one 5-st I-Cord 6"/15cm in length. Join ends, forming a circle, then twist into double circle and slip onto end of two cords above the knots.

cardigan shawl collar

▲▶ With RS facing and circular needle, pick up sts along right front, pm for start of neck shaping, pick up sts around neck, pm at end of neck shaping, pick up sts down left front. Work in garter st for 9 rows, making buttonholes on 5th row of right front.

Short rows Knit to within 2 sts of 2nd neck marker, wrap and turn (w&t) as foll: sl 1, bring yarn to front, sl same st back to LH needle, turn work. Knit to within 2 sts of next marker, w&t. Rep last 2 rows 3 more times, working 2 less sts each time.

Next row Knit across row, knitting wrap at every short row tog with corresponding st on needle. Knit last row on all sts, knitting wrap with corresonding st on needle. Bind off.

Sew buttons opposite buttonholes.

saw tooth eyelet v-neck/floral

▶ Cast on 6 sts.

Row 1 K3, yo, k3—7 sts.

Rows 2, 4, 6, 8 and 10 Knit.

Row 3 K3, yo, k4—8 sts.

Row 5 K3, yo, k5—9 sts

Row 7 K3, yo, k6—10 sts.

Row 9 K3, yo, k7—11 sts.

Row 11 K3 yo, k8—12 sts.

Row 12 Bind off 6 sts, k5—6 sts.

Rep rows 1–12 to desired length.

Bind off.

Sew straight edge of saw tooth edging to neck edge.

Run ribbon through eyelet row leaving 2 long ends at center front.

flower

Make a length of 8 saw tooth pats.

Twist length into a spiral and sew at back to hold spiral in place.

Sew flower to V-neck.

Sew beads in center of flower and 2 lengths of ribbon extending from flower.

crewneck/cord

▲ With RS facing, pick up an even number of sts around neck edge. Work in 1x1 rib for 1"/2.6cm. Bind off.

▶ **cords**

Make one 2-st I-Cord (see page 154) to fit around neck edge. Bind off and sew around to bound-off neck edge. Make one 3-st I-Cord to fit around first row of neck edge. Bind off and sew around to first row of neck edge. Make one long 3-st I-Cord allowing 4"/10cm for each loop and place sts on a holder. Create graduating loops with cord and adjust for length. Bind off and sew in position.

rib turtleneck/eyelet/cord tie

▲ With RS facing, pick up a multiple of 4 sts around neck edge. Work in 2x2 rib for 5"/12.5cm.

Eyelet row *K1, p2tog, yo, k1; rep from * to end.

Cont in 2x2 rib for 1"/2.5cm. Bind off.

▶ **cord**

Make one 5-st I-Cord (see page 154) approximately 20"/50cm long. Fold turtleneck down. Thread cord through eyelet row and tie in front.

mandarin collar/frog closure

▲ Cast on desired number of sts.

Work in St st for 1½"/4cm.

Purl next RS row for turning ridge.

Purl next row.

Cont in St st for 1½"/4 cm.

Bind off.

Fold collar in half along turning ridge and sew to neck edge with opening in the front.

▶ **frog closure**

Make two 3-st I-Cords (see page 154) approximately 10"/2.5cm in length.

Follow diagram to form two sides of frog closure, one with a knot at the end and one with a loop at the end.

Attach each side of frog closure to mandarin collar.

•start

1x1 rib/braid center

▶ Cast on 21 sts.

Work in 1x1 rib for 6"/15cm.

Next row *Rib 7, join another strand of yarn; rep from * once, rib 7.

Work each strip separately for 6"/15cm.

Braid these three separate pieces together.

Joining row With first strand of yarn, rib across all 21 sts dropping other strands of yarn. Cont in rib in one piece for 6"/12.5 cm.

Bind off.

garter neck/elegant scrolled cord

▲ With RS facing, pick up sts around neck edge.

Work in garter st for 4"/10 cm.

Bind off.

▶ **scroll**

Make two 3-st I-Cords (see page 154)

approximately 20"/50cm length.

Follow diagram to form two separate scrolls.

Sew scroll in position.

• start
• end

scalloped garter round neck

▲ Cast on 123 sts (or a multiple of 11 sts plus 2).

Row 1 Knit.

Row 2 K2, *k1, sl this st back to LH needle, with RH needle lift the next 8 sts one at a time over this st and off needle, [yo] twice, k first st again, k2; rep from * to end.

Row 3 K1, *p2tog, [k1, p1, k1, p1] in double yo, p1; rep from *, end k1.

Work in garter st until desired length.

Bind off.

Sew to neck edge.

halter neck/florals

▲ Cast on desired number of sts.

Work in garter st for 1"/2.5cm.

Bind off.

flowers

Colors A and B

With A or B, cast on 57 sts.

Row 1 (WS) Purl.

Row 2 K2, *k1, sl this st back to LH needle, with RH needle lift the next 8 sts one at a time over this st and off needle, [yo] twice, k first st again, k2; rep from * to end—27 sts.

Row 3 P1, *p2tog, [k1, p1, k1, p1] in double yo, p1; rep from *, end p1—32 sts.

Row 4 K1, *k3tog; rep from *, end k1—12 sts.

Row 5 [P2tog] 6 times—6 sts. Sl 2nd, 3rd, 4th, 5th and 6th st over first st.

Fasten off.

Sew seam.

Attach beads to center of flower.

Sew flowers to halter neck.

v-neck vertical 1x1 rib

▶ Cast on 8 sts.

Work in 1x1 rib until piece reaches around
entire neck edge.

Bind off.

Sew rib to neck overlapping left front over
right front at V.

Add fur trim to edge of ribbing.

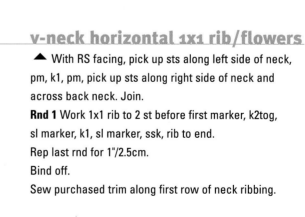

v-neck horizontal 1x1 rib/flowers

▲ With RS facing, pick up sts along left side of neck,
pm, k1, pm, pick up sts along right side of neck and
across back neck. Join.

Rnd 1 Work 1x1 rib to 2 st before first marker, k2tog,
sl marker, k1, sl marker, ssk, rib to end.

Rep last rnd for 1"/2.5cm.

Bind off.

Sew purchased trim along first row of neck ribbing.

2x2 rib with 6-st cable

▲ Cast on 50 sts.

Row 1 K2, *p2, k2; rep from * to end.

Row 2 P2, *k2, p2; rep from * to end.

Rep rows 1 and 2 for 5"/12.5cm.

Bind off.

▶ **6-st cable**

Cast on 6 sts.

Rows 1, 3 and 5 K6.

Rows 2, 4, 6 and 8 P6.

Row 7 Sl 3 sts to cn and hold in front, k3, then k3 from cn.

Rep rows 1–8 for 20"/50cm.

Bind off.

Center narrow ends of 6-st cable piece to side edges of 2x2 rib piece. Sew in place.

rib/balls

▲ With RS facing, pick up 76 sts (or a multiple of 4 sts) around neck edge.

Work in 2x2 rib for 6"/15cm.

Bind off.

▲ **balls**

(make 6)

Cast on 8 sts, leaving a long tail for seaming.

Row 1 K in front and back of every st—16 sts.

Row 2 and all WS rows Purl.

Rows 3, 5, 7 and 9 Knit.

Row 11 K2tog to end—8 sts.

With tapestry needle run thread through 8 sts and gather, securing thread. Run cast-on tail through cast-on sts and gather, securing thread. Stuff with fiberfill. Sew side edges together.

Attach 6 balls evenly spaced around front of turtleneck 1"/2.5cm above bound-off edge.

corners

st st fold hem

▲ Cast on desired number of sts.

Work in St st for 1"/2.5cm.

Purl next RS row for turning ridge.

Purl next row.

Cont in St st for desired length.

Turn hem to WS along turning ridge and sew in place.

Lace

Sew on at turning ridge.

Beads

Sew on at turning ridge.

Fur

Sew on at turning ridge.

lattice beauty

▲ Cast on 44 sts (or a multiple of 6 sts plus 2).

PW2 P1 wrapping yarn twice around needle.

3-st LC Sl 1 st to cn and hold to front, k2, k1 from cn.

3-st RC Sl 2 sts to cn and hold to back, k1, k2 from cn.

Note on rows 2 and 8 Drop extra wrap to make elongated st.

Row 1 (WS) P1, PW2, p4, *[PW2] twice, p4; rep from *, end PW2, p1.

Row 2 K1, sl 1, k4, *sl 2, k4; rep from *, end sl 1, k1.

Row 3 P1, sl 1, p4, *sl 2, p4; rep from *, end sl 1, p1.

Rows 4 and 5 Rep rows 2 and 3.

Row 6 K1, *3-st LC, 3-st RC; rep from *, end k1.

Row 7 P3, [PW2] twice, *p4, [PW2] twice; rep from *, end p3.

Row 8 K3, sl 2, *k4, sl 2; rep from *, end k3.

Row 9 P3, sl 2, *p4, sl 2; rep from *, end p3.

Rows 10 and 11 Rep rows 8 and 9.

Row 12 K1, *3-st RC, 3-st LC; rep from *, end k1.

corner

Next row (WS) Cont in lattice beauty pattern (rows 1–12) on first 12 sts, then p to end.

Next row K to last 12 sts, then cont lattice beauty pattern on last 12 sts.

Cont as established in lattice beauty pattern on 12 sts and St st on remaining sts until desired length.

& edges

ball 'n cable cord front band

▶▲ **balls** (make 4 or desired number)

Cast on 10 sts, leaving a long tail for seaming.

4-st LC Sl 2 sts to cn and hold in front, k2, then k2 from cn.

Rows 1, 3 and 5 (RS) Knit.

Rows 2, 4, 6 and 8 Purl.

Row 7 *K3tog, k2tog; rep from * to end—4 sts.

Row 9 4-st LC.

Rows 10–12 Work in St st.

Rows 13–20 Rep rows 9–12 twice more, leaving sts on needle on last row. Stuff each ball with fiberfill. Sew edges together.

Join balls

Row 1 (RS) K4 from first ball 'n cable, *cast on 4 sts, k4 sts from next ball 'n cable; rep from * across all balls.

Rows 2 and 4 *P4, k4; rep from *, end p4.

Row 3 *4-st LC, p4; rep from *, end 4-st LC.

Rows 5 and 7 *K4, p4; rep from *, end k4.

Rows 6 and 8 *P4, k4; rep from *, end p4.

corner

Next row (WS) P to last 4 sts, then work cable pat (rows 9–12).

Next row Cont cable pat on 4 sts, k to end.

Cont as established in cable pattern on 4 sts and St st on remaining sts until desired length.

victory blocks

▲ Cast on 29 sts. (make 2)

K2TW2 Knit 2 sts tog, wrapping yarn twice around needle.
On next row, [k1, p1] in the double yo.

Row 1 (WS) Purl.

Row 2 Knit.

Row 3 P3, *[K2TW2] 5 times, p3; rep from * once.

Row 4 K3, *[k1, p1] 5 times, k3; rep from * once.

Row 5 P3, k1, [K2TW2] 4 times, p5, [K2TW2] 4 times, k1, p3.

Row 6 K4, *[k1, p1] 4 times, k5, [k1, p1] 4 times, k4.

Row 7 P3, [K2TW2] 4 times, p7, [K2TW2] 4 times, p3.

Row 8 K3, [k1, p1] 4 times, k7, [k1, p1] 4 times, k3.

Row 9 P3, k1 [K2TW2] 3 times, p9, [K2TW2] 3 times, k1, p3.

Row 10 K4, [k1, p1] 3 times, k9, [k1, p1] 3 times, k4.

Row 11 P3, [K2TW2] 3 times, p11, [K2TW2] 3 times, p3.

Row 12 K3, [k1, p1] 3 times, k11, [k1, p1] 3 times, k3.

Row 13 P3, k1, [K2TW2] twice, p 13, [K2TW2] twice, k1, p3.

Row 14 K5, p1, k1, p1, k14, p1, k1, p1, k4.

Row 15 P3, [K2TW2] twice, p15, [K2TW2] twice, p3.

Row 16 K4, p1, k1, p1, k16, p1, k1, p1, k3.

Row 17 P3, k1, K2TW2, p17, K2TW2, k1, p3.

Row 18 K5, p1, k18, p1, k4.

Row 19 P3, K2TW2, p19, K2TW2, p3.

Row 20 K4, p1, k20, p1, k3.

Place sts on a holder.

Joining row (WS) P29 sts of first block, then p29 sts of next block.

Cont in St st until desired length.

st st casing and drawstring

▲ Cast on desired number of sts.

Work in St st for 1"/2.5cm.

Purl next RS row for turning ridge.

Purl next row.

Cont in St st for 1"/2.5cm.

Drawstring opening (RS) K to center 4 sts, bind off 4 center sts, k to end.

Next row Purl, casting on 4 sts over bound-off sts.

Cont in St st until desired length.

Turn hem to WS along turning ridge and sew in place.

cord

Make a 4-st I-Cord (see page 154) until desired length.

Thread cord through eyelet row and tie in front.

garter cup corner and flowers

▶▲ (beg with 7 sts and end with a multiple of 14 sts)

First strip Cast on 7 sts.

Work in garter st for 3"/7.5cm.

Cut yarn and leave sts on needle.

On same needle, cast on and work as before to make another strip.

Cont in this manner until desired number of strips are made
(each strip will make 14 sts).

Join strips *K7, with RS facing, k7 from cast-on edge; rep from * to
last strip.

Cont in garter st for 3"/7.5cm.

Next row (RS) Knit across.

Next row K7, p to end.

Rep last 2 rows until desired length.

le fleur

Cast on 40 sts.

Row 1 (WS) *K1, bind off 6 sts (2 more sts on RH needle);
rep from * to end—10 sts.

Run threaded tapestry needle through rem sts on needle,
pull tightly and secure. Cont in this manner until desired number of
flowers are made.

Sew flowers to background.

alice's drawstring lace

▶ Cast on 13 sts.

Row 1 K3, yo, k2tog, k1, (yo twice, k2tog) 3 times, k1—16 sts.

Row 2 K3, [p1, k2] 3 times, k4.

Row 3 K3, yo, k2tog, k11—16 sts.

Row 4 Bind off 3 sts, k to end—13 sts.

Rep rows 1–4 for 12"/30.5cm or desired length.

Bind off.

Thread ribbon through eyelets on garter st edge.

double v's with ribbon bows

▶ Cast on 30 sts (or a multiple of 30 sts).

Row 1 (RS) Knit.

Row 2 and all WS rows Knit.

Row 3 K6, [yo, k2tog] 11 times, yo, k2.

Row 5 K9, [yo, k2tog] 10 times, yo, k2.

Row 7 K12, [yo, k2tog] 9 times, yo, k2.

Row 9 K15, [yo, k2tog] 8 times, yo, k2.

Row 11 K18, [yo, k2tog] 7 times, yo, k2.

Row 13 K15, [yo, k2tog] 9 times, yo, k2.

Row 15 K12, [yo, k2tog] 11 times, yo, k2.

Row 17 K9, [yo, k2tog] 13 times, yo, k2.

Row 19 K6, [yo, k2tog] 15 times, yo, k2.

Row 21 Knit.

Row 22 Bind off 9 sts loosely, k to end.

Rep rows 1–22 until desired length.

Bind off.

Tie ribbons through eyelets at garter st edge.

eyelet mitered corner

▼ This eyelet corner is worked on 11 sts, using the center st as the axis of the angle. It is knitted from the inside outward.

Row 1 (RS) K5, yo, k1, yo, k5.

Row 2 K to center st, p1, k to end.

Row 3 K to center st, yo, k1, yo, k to end.

Rep rows 2 and 3 until desired width.

Bind off.

garter st mitered corner

▼ This mitered corner is worked from the inside outward on 11 sts, using the center st as the axis of the angle.

Row 1 (RS) K5, M1, k1, M1, k5.

Row 2 K to center st, p1, k to end.

Row 3 K to center st, M1, k1, M1, k to end.

Rep rows 2 and 3 until desired width

Bind off.

single angle-line mitered corner

▼ This mitered corner is worked on 11 sts, from the inside outward.

Row 1 (RS) K5, M1, k1, M1, k5.

Row 2 Purl.

Row 3 K to center st, M1, k1, M1, k to end.

Rep rows 2 and 3 until desired width.

Bind off.

double angle-line mitered corner

▼ This mitered corner is worked from the inside outward on 11 sts, using the center st as the axis of the angle.

Row 1 (RS) K4, k in front and back of next st, k3, k in back and front of next st, k4.

Row 2 Purl.

Row 3 K to center 3 sts, k into the next st in the row below, k3, k into the st below the last worked st, k to end.

Rep rows 2 and 3 until desired width.

Bind off.

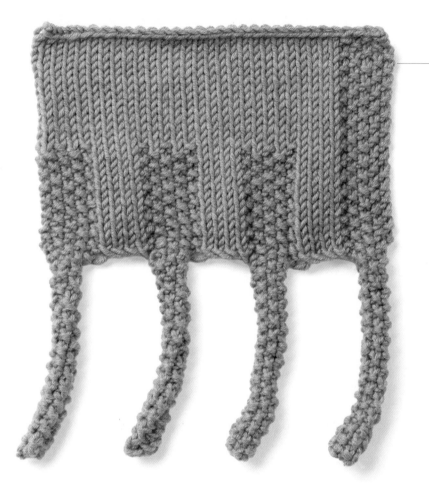

seed st cord/front band

▶▲ **cords** (make desired number)

Cast on 5 sts. *Work 5 seed sts. Do not turn. Slide sts to right end of needle. Pull yarn to tighten. Rep from * for 4"/10cm.

Rep for desired number of cords leaving sts on needle.

Join cords

Row 1 (RS) Work 5 seed sts of first cord, *cast on 5 sts, work 5 seed sts of next cord; rep from * across all cords.

Row 2 *Work 5 seed sts, p5; rep from *, end 5 seed sts.

Row 3 *Work 5 seed sts, k5; rep from *, end 5 seed sts.

Rep rows 2 and 3 for 2"/5cm.

Next row (RS) Work 5 seed sts, k to end.

Next row P to last 5 sts, work 5 seed sts.

Rep last 2 rows until desired length.

Loop, knot or twist the cords when done.

looped cords

Sew cast-on edge of first cord behind top of 2nd cord. Rep this across all loops.

Sew last loop to seam.

knotted cords

Tie a knot a bottom of one cord, then at top of next cord alternately.

twisted cords

Twist each set of two cords together and sew in place.

vertical/horizontal pucker stitch

▲ **Colors** A and B

With A, cast on 32 sts (or a multiple of 21 sts plus 11).

Preparation row With A, purl.

Row 1 (RS) With B, [k1, sl 1] 5 times, *k12, sl 1, [k1, sl 1] 4 times; rep from *, end k1.

Row 2 With B, [p1, sl 1] 5 times, *p12, sl 1, [p1, sl 1] 4 times; rep from *, end p1.

Row 3 With A, k2, sl 1, [k1, sl 1] 3 times, *k14, sl 1, [k1, sl 1] 3 times; rep from *, end k2.

Row 4 With A, p2, sl 1, [p1, sl 1] 3 times, *p14, sl 1, [p1, sl 1] 3 times; rep from *, end p2.

Rep rows 1–4 for 3"/7.5cm or until desired length.

Next row (RS) Purl.

Cont in St st until desired length.

petite quercus points

(worked over 16 sts)

Preparation row Purl.

Row 1 (WS) K1, p to last st, k1.

Row 2 K2tog, k to last 2 sts, k2tog—14 sts.

Row 3 Rep row 1.

Row 4 *K2tog, yo; rep from * to last 4 sts, k2tog twice—12 sts.

Row 5 Knit.

Row 6 K2tog, k to last 2 sts, k2tog—10 sts.

Rep rows 1–6 once more, then rows 1 and 2 once—2 sts.

P2tog. Fasten off.

6 petite points

▸ Cast on 96 sts.

Next row (RS) K16 sts for first point, leaving rem 80 sts on hold for 2nd through 6th points.

Work first point.

Return to sts on hold and work 2nd point on next 16 sts.

Cont in this manner working 3rd through 6th points on each set of 16 sts.

quercus point

▲ (worked over 32 sts)

Preparation row Purl.

Row 1 (WS) K1, p to last st, k1.

Row 2 K2tog, k to last 2 sts, k2tog—30 sts.

Row 3 Rep row 1.

Row 4 *K2tog, yo; rep from * to last 4 sts, k2tog twice—28 sts.

Row 5 Knit.

Row 6 K2tog, k to last 2 sts, k2tog—26 sts.

Rep rows 1–6 four more times—2 sts.

P2tog. Fasten off.

2 points

▶ Cast on 64 sts.

Work in St st for 1"/2.5cm.

Next row (RS) K32 sts for the first point, leaving rem 32 sts on hold for 2nd point.

Work first point.

Return to sts on holder and work 2nd point.

victorian lace

▶ Cast on 14 sts.

Row 1 (WS) K2, yo, k2tog, k5, yo, k2tog, yo, k3—15 sts.

Row 2 and all RS rows K1, yo, k2tog, k to end.

Row 3 K2, yo, k2tog, k4, [yo, k2tog] twice, yo, k3—16 sts.

Row 5 K2, yo, k2tog, k3, [yo, k2tog] 3 times, yo, k3—17 sts.

Row 7 K2, yo, k2tog, k2, [yo, k2tog] 4 times, yo, k3—18 sts.

Row 9 K2, yo, k2tog, k1, [yo, k2tog] 5 times, yo, k3—19 sts.

Row 11 K2, yo, k2tog, k1, k2tog, [yo, k2tog] 5 times, k2—18 sts.

Row 13 K2, yo, k2tog, k2, k2tog, [yo, k2tog] 4 times, k2—17 sts.

Row 15 K2, yo, k2tog, k3, k2tog, [yo, k2tog] 3 times, k2—16 sts.

Row 17 K2, yo, k2tog, k4, k2tog, [yo, k2tog] twice, k2—15 sts.

Row 19 K2, yo, k2tog, k5, k2tog, yo, k2tog, k2—14 sts.

Row 20 Rep row 2.

Rep rows 1–20 until desired length to corner, end with pat row 9.

Turn corner

Short row 1 (RS) K1, yo, k2tog, k to last 5 sts, sl 1, turn, k to end.

Short row 2 (RS) K1, yo, k2tog, k to last 7 sts, sl 1, turn, k to end.

Short row 3 (RS) K1, yo, k2tog, k to last 9 sts, sl 1, turn, k to end.

Short row 4 (RS) K1, yo, k2tog, k to last 11 sts, sl 1, turn, k to end.

Short row 5 (RS) K1, yo, k2tog, k to last 13 sts, sl 1, turn, k to end.

Short rows 6 and 7 (RS) K1, yo, k2tog, sl 1, turn, k to end.

Short row 8 (RS) K1, yo, k2tog, k1, sl 1, turn, k to end.

Short row 9 (RS) K1, yo, k2tog, k3, sl 1, turn, k to end.

Short row 10 (RS) K1, yo, k2tog, k5, sl 1, turn, k to end.

Short row 11 (RS) K1, yo, k2tog, k7, sl 1, turn, k to end.

Short row 12 (RS) K1, yo, k2tog, k9, sl 1, turn, k to end.

Beg with pat row 10, cont to work in Victorian lace pattern to next corner, then turn corner again. Cont in this manner until border is completed.

running scallop

▶ Cast on 11 sts.

Row 1 K5, p4, [p1, k1] in next st, p1—12 sts.
Row 2 SK2P, M1, SKP, M1, k1 tbl, M1, k2tog, k4—11 sts.
Row 3 K5, p4, [p1, k1] in next st, p1—12 sts.
Row 4 SK2P, M1, k1 tbl, [M1, k3] twice, k2—13 sts.
Row 5 K5, p6, [p1, k1] in next st, p1—14 sts.
Row 6 SK2P, M1, k1 tbl, M1, k2tog, k1, SKP, M1, k5—13 sts.
Row 7 K5, p6, [p1, k1] in next st, p1—14 sts.
Row 8 SK2P, M1, k1 tbl, M1, k2tog, k1, SKP, M1, k5—13 sts.
Row 9 K5, p6, [p1, k1] in next st, p1—14 sts.
Row 10 SK2P, M1, SKP, M1, SK2P, M1, k2tog, k4—11 sts.
Rep rows 1–10 until desired length.

angel lace

▶ Cast on 9 sts.

Row 1 and all RS rows Knit.
Row 2 K3, [k2tog, yo] twice, k1, yo, k1—10 sts.
Row 4 K2, [k2tog, yo] twice, k3, yo, k1—11 sts.
Row 6 K1, [k2tog, yo] twice, k5, yo, k1—12 sts.
Row 8 K3, [yo, k2tog] twice, k1, k2tog, yo, k2tog—11 sts.
Row 10 K4, yo, k2tog, yo, k3tog, yo, k2tog—10 sts.
Row 12 K5, yo, k3tog, yo, k2tog—9 sts.
Rep rows 1–12 until desired length to corner,
ending with pat row 6.

Turn corner
Row 1 K10, turn.
Row 2 Sl 1, [yo, k2tog] twice, k1, k2tog, yo, k2tog.
Row 3 K8, turn.
Row 4 Sl 1, yo, k2tog, yo, k3tog, yo, k2tog.
Row 5 K6, turn.
Row 6 Sl 1, yo, k3tog, yo, k2tog.
Row 7 K6, turn.
Row 8 [K2tog, yo] twice, k1, yo, k1.

Row 9 K8, turn.
Row 10 [K2tog, yo] twice, k3, yo, k1.
Row 11 K10, turn.
Row 12 [K2tog, yo] twice, k5, yo, k1.
Row 13 K to end.

Beg with pat row 8, cont to work in angel lace pattern to next corner, then turn corner again. Cont in this manner until border is completed.

cambridge muse

▲ Cast on 37 sts (or a multiple of 18 sts plus 19).

Row 1 (WS) K2, p3, k9, p3, *k3, p3, k9, p3; rep from * to last 2 sts, k2.

Row 2 P2tog, k3, M1p, p9, M1p, k3, *p3tog, k3, M1p, p9, M1p, k3; rep from *, end p2tog.

Row 3 K1, *p3, k11, p3, k1; rep from * to end.

Row 4 P1, *M1p, k3, p2tog, p7, p2tog, k3, M1p, p1; rep from * to end.

Row 5 K2, p3, k9, p3, *k3, p3, k9, p3; rep from *, end, k2.

Row 6 P2, M1p, k3, p2tog, p5, p2tog, k3, M1p, *p3, M1p, k3, p2tog, p5, p2tog, k3, M1p; rep from *, end p2.

Row 7 K3, p3, k7, p3, *k5, p3, k7, p3; rep from *, end k3.

Row 8 P3, M1p, k3, p2tog, p3, p2tog, k3, M1p, *p5, M1p, k3, p2tog, p3, p2tog, k3, M1p; rep from *, end p3.

Row 9 K4, p3, k5, p3, *k7, p3, k5, p3; rep from *, end k4.

Row 10 P4, M1p, k3, p2tog, p1, p2tog, k3, M1p, *p7, M1p, k3, p2tog, p1, p2tog, k3, M1p; rep from *, end p4.

Row 11 K5, p3, k3, p3, *k9, p3, k3, p3; rep from *, end k5.

Row 12 P5, M1p, k3, p3tog, k3, M1p, *p9, M1p, k3, p3tog, k3, M1p; rep from *, end p5.

Row 13 K6, p3, k1, p3, *k11, p3, k1, p3; rep from *, end k6.

Row 14 P4, p2tog, k3, M1p, p1, M1p, k3, p2tog, *p7, p2tog, k3, M1p, p1, M1p, k3, p2tog; rep from *, end p4.

Row 15 Rep row 11.

Row 16 P3, p2tog, k3, M1p, p3, M1p, k3, p2tog, *p5, p2tog, k3, M1p, p3, M1p, k3, p2tog; rep from *, end p3.

Row 17 Rep row 9.

Row 18 P2, p2tog, k3, M1p, p5, M1p, k3, p2tog, *p3, p2tog, k3, M1p, p5, M1p, k3, p2tog; rep from *, end p2.

Row 19 Rep row 7.

Row 20 P1, *p2tog, k3, M1p, p7, M1p, k3, p2tog, p1; rep from * to end.

Row 21 Rep row 5.

Row 22 P2tog, k3, M1p, p9, M1p, k3, *p3tog, k3, M1p, p9, M1p, k3; rep from *, end p2tog.

Row 23 K1, *p3, k11, p3, k1; rep from * to end.

Cont in garter st.

Sew purchased lion medallions along cast-on edge.

tree tops

▲ Cast on 47 sts (or a multiple of 15 sts plus 2) .

Row 1 (WS) P2, *M1, k3, p2, p3tog, p2, k3, M1, p2, rep from * to end.

Row 2 K2, *p4, k5, p4, k2, rep from * to end.

Row 3 P2, *M1, k4, p1, p3tog, p1, k4, M1, p2, rep from * to end.

Row 4 K2, *p5, k3, p5, k2, rep from * to end.

Row 5 P2, *M1, k5, p3tog, k5, M1, p2, rep from * to end.

Row 6 K2, *p6, k1, p6, k2, rep from * to end.

Rep rows 1–6 once more.

corner

Next row (WS) P to last 15 sts, then work tree top pat (rows 1–6).

Next row Cont tree top pat on first 15 sts, k to end.

Cont as established in tree top pattern on 15 sts and rem sts in St st until desired length.

Make bobbles and attach to points at lower edge, either singly, as shown, or in clusters.

MB (make bobble) Cast on 1 st, leaving a 4"/10cm tail. K in front, back, front, back and front of same st (5 sts made in one st). Turn. P 1 row, k 1 row, p 1 row.

Next row K2tog, k1, k2tog—3 sts. SP2P. Fasten off, leaving 4"/10cm tail. Fold bobble in half and pull both tails through to WS of finished piece, knot them tog.

chevron classic

▲ **Colors** A, B and C

With A, cast on 39 sts (or a multiple of 12 sts plus 3)

Row 1 (RS) K1, ssk, *k9, SK2P; rep from * to last 12 sts, k9, k2tog, k1.

Row 2 K1, *p1, k4, [k1, yo, k1] in next st, k4; rep from *, end p1, k1.

Rep rows 1 and 2 in the following color sequence: 2 rows each with B, C and A, 4 rows with B, then 2 rows with C.

corner

Next row (RS) With A, k to last 15 sts, then work chevron classic pat (rows 1–2).

Next row Cont chevron classic pat on first 15 sts, then with A p to end.

Cont as established in chevron classic pattern on 15 sts working 2 rows each of B, C and A and rem sts in St st with A only until desired length.

& edges

tweed checks

▲ **Colors** A and B.

With A, cast on 39 sts (or a multiple of 10 sts plus 9).

Row 1 (RS) Knit.

Rows 2–4 Work in St st.

Row 5 With B, k1, sl 1 wyib, k1, sl 3 wyib, *[k1, sl 1 wyib] 3 times, k1, sl 3 wyib; rep from *, end k1, sl 1 wyib, k1.

Row 6 With B, k1, sl 1 wyif, k1, sl 3 wyif, *[k1, sl 1 wyif] 3 times, k1, sl 3 wyif; rep from *, end k1, sl 1 wyif, k1.

Rows 7 and 8 With A work 2 rows in St st.

Rows 9–18 Rep rows 5–8 twice more, then rows 5 and 6 again.

corner

Next row (RS) With A, p to last 13 sts, sl 3 wyib, then cont tweed checks pat.

Next row Cont tweed checks pat on first 10 sts, then with A k to end.

Cont as established in tweed checks pat on 10 sts and reverse St st with A on rem sts slipping the 3 sts every other row until desired length.

woven block stitch

▲ **Colors** A and B

With A, cast on 40 sts (or a multiple of 9 sts plus 4).

Work 3 rows in St st, end with a RS row.

K next WS row for turning ridge.

Row 1 (RS) With A, knit.

Row 2 With A, purl.

Row 3 With B, k1, *sl 2 wyib, k1, [sl 1 wyif, k1] 3 times; rep from *, end sl 2 wyib, k1.

Row 4 With B, k1, *sl 2 wyif, p7; rep from *, end sl 2 wyif, k1.

Row 5 With A, k3, *sl 1 wyif, [k1, sl 1 wyif] 3 times, k2; rep from *, end k1.

Row 6 With A, purl.

Row 7–14 Rep rows 3–6 twice more.

Rep rows 1–14.

corner

Next row (RS) With B k to last 12 sts, then work woven block stitch pat (rows 1–14).

Next row Cont woven block stitch pat on first 12 sts, then with B p to end.

Cont as established in woven block stitch pat on 12 sts and St st with B on rem sts until desired length.

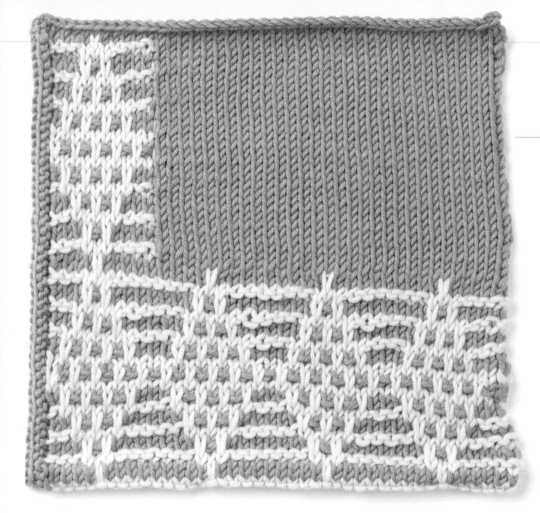

dotted diamonds

▲ **Colors** A and B

With B, cast on 41 sts (or a multiple of 10 sts plus 1).

Work in St st for 1"/2.5cm for hem, end with a WS row.

With A, knit 2 rows.

Row 1 (RS) With B, k5, *sl 1 wyib, k9, rep from *, end sl 1 wyib, k5.

Row 2 With B, p5, *sl 1 wyif, p9, rep from *, end sl 1 wyif, p5.

Row 3 With A, knit.

Row 4 With A, k4, *p3, k7, rep from *, end p3, k4.

Row 5 With B, k4, *sl 1, k1, sl 1 wyib, k7, rep from *, end last rep k4.

Row 6 With B, p4, *sl 1, k1, sl 1 wyif, p7, rep from *, end last rep p4.

Row 7 With A, knit.

Row 8 With A, k3, *p5, k5, rep from *, end p5, k3.

Row 9 With B, k3, *(sl 1 wyib, k1) twice, sl 1 wyib, k5, rep from *, end last rep k3.

Row 10 With B, p3, *(sl 1 wyif, k1) twice, sl 1 wyif, p5, rep from *, end last rep p3.

Row 11 With A, knit.

Row 12 With A, k2, *p7, k3, rep from *, end p7, k2.

Row 13 With B, k2, *(sl 1 wyib, k1) 3 times, sl 1 wyib, k3, rep from *, end last rep k2.

Row 14 With B, p2, *(sl 1 wyif, k1) 3 times, sl 1 wyif, p3, rep from *, end last rep p2.

Row 15 With A, knit.

Row 16 With A, purl.

Row 17 With B, k1, *sl 1 wyib, k1, rep from * to end.

Row 18 With B, k1, *sl 1 wyif, k1, rep from * to end.

Rows 19 and 20 With A, rep rows 15 and 16.

Rows 21 and 22 With B, rep rows 13 and 14.

Rows 23 and 24 With A, rep rows 11 and 12.

Rows 25 and 26 With B, rep rows 9 and 10.

Rows 27 and 28 With A, rep rows 7 and 8.

Rows 29 and 30 With B, rep rows 5 and 6.

Rows 31 and 32 With A, rep rows 3 and 4.

corner

Next row (RS) With B, k to last 10 sts, cont row 1 of dotted diamonds pat.

Next row Cont dotted diamonds pat on 10 sts, then with B p to end.

Cont as established in dotted diamonds pat on 10 sts and St st with B on rem sts until desired length.

Fold along turning ridge and sew hem to WS.

Front band edging

With RS facing and A, pick up desired amount of sts along front edge. Knit 1 row. Bind off.

& edges

cable block corner

▲ Cast on 28 sts (or a multiple of 18 sts plus 10).

Knit 2 rows.

RT Knit 2nd st on LH needle, k first st on LH needle, sl both sts from needle tog.

Row 1 (RS) *[P1, RT] 3 times, p1, k8 tbl; rep from *, end [p1, RT] 3 times, p1.

Row 2 *[K1, p2] 3 times, k1, p8 tbl, rep from *, end last rep k1.

Rep rows 1 and 2 four times more.

corner

***Row 1 (RS)** P to last 10 sts, p1, k8 tbl, p1.

Row 2 K1, p8 tbl, k1, k to end.

Rows 8–10 Rep rows 1 and 2 four times more.

Row 11 P to last 10 sts, [p1, RT] 3 times, p1.

Row 12 K1, [p2, k1] 3 times; k to end.*

Rep rows 11 and 12 four times more.*

Rep from * to *.

Cont as established in cable block corner pattern on 10 sts and St st on rem sts until desired length.

embossed leaf stitch

▲ Cast on 28 sts (or a multiple of 7 sts).

Row 1 (WS) Knit.

Row 2 Purl.

Row 3 Knit.

Row 4 *P3, k1, p3; rep from * to end.

Row 5 *K3, [p in front, back and front] of next st, k3; rep from *.

Row 6 *P3, k3, p3; rep from *.

Row 7 *K3, [p in front and back] of next st, p1, [p in front and back] next st, k3; rep from *.

Row 8 *P3, k5, k3; rep from *.

Row 9 *K3, [p in front and back] of next st, p3, [p in front and back] of next st, k3; rep from *.

Row 10 *P3, k7, p3; rep from *.

Row 11 *K3, [p in front and back] of next st, p5, [p in front and back of next st, k3; rep from *.

Row 12 *P3, k9, p3; rep from *.

Row 13 *K3, p2tog, p5, p2tog tbl, k3; rep from *.

Row 14 *P3, k7, p3; rep from *.

Row 15 *K3, p2tog, p3, p2tog tbl, k3; rep from *.

Row 16 *P3, k5, p3; rep from *.

Row 17 *K3, p2tog, p1, p2tog tbl, k3; rep from *.

Row 18 *P3, k3, p3; rep from *.

Row 19 *K3, p3tog, k3; rep from *.

Row 20 *P3, k1, p3; rep from *.

corner

Next row (RS) K to last 7 sts, work embossed diamond stitch pat (rows 1–20).

Next row Cont embossed diamond stitch pat on first 7 sts, then p to end.

Cont as established in embossed diamond stitch pattern on 7 sts and St st on rem sts until desired length.

lotus and pillar

▲ Cast on 55 sts (or a multiple of 26 sts plus 3).
Work 3 rows St st.

PS (pillar st) Working over the next 3 sts: Yo, k3, pass yo over the 3 k sts.

Row 1 (WS) *P3, k11, p1, k11; rep from *, end p3.

Row 2 (RS) *PS, p11, k1 tbl, p11; rep from *, end PS.

Row 3 *P3, k11, p1, k11; rep from *, end p3.

Row 4 *K3, p11, k1 tbl, p11; rep from *, end k3.

Row 5 *P3, k11, p1, k11; rep from *, end p3.

Row 6 *PS, p11, [k1, p1, k1] in next st, p11; rep from *, end PS.

Row 7 *P3, k11, p3, k11; rep from *, end p3.

Row 8 *K3, p9, p2tog, [k1 tbl, k1] in next st, k1, [k1 tbl, k1] in next st, p2tog, p9; rep from *, end k3.

Row 9 *P3, k10, p5, k10; rep from *, end p3.

Row 10 *PS, p6, [p2tog] twice, ([k1 tbl, k1] in next st) twice, k1, ([k1 tbl, k1] in next st) twice, [p2tog] twice, p6; rep from *, end PS.

Row 11 *P3, k8, p9, k8; rep from *, end p3.

Row 12 *K3, [p2tog] 4 times, ([k1 tbl, k1] in next st) 4 times, k1, ([k1 tbl, k1] in next st) 4 times, [p2tog] 4 times; rep from *, end k3.

Row 13 *P3, k4, p17, k4; rep from *, end p3.

Row 14 *PS, p2, p2tog, [k1 tbl, k1] in next st, k15, [k1 tbl, k1] in next st, p2tog, p2; rep from*; end PS.

Row 15 *P3, k3, p19, k3; rep from *, end p3.

Row 16 *K3, p3, [k3, p1] 4 times, k3, p3; rep from *, end k3.

Row 17 *P3, k3, [p3, k1] 4 times, p3, k3; rep from *, end p3.

Row 18 *PS, p3, [k3, p1] 4 times, k3, p3; rep from *, end PS.

Row 19 *P3, k3, [p3, k1] 4 times, p3, k3; rep from *, end p3.

Row 20 *K3, p3, (k3, [k1 tbl, k1] in next st) 4 times, k3, p3; rep from *, end k3.

Row 21 *P3, k3, p3, k1, ([p1, p1 tbl] in next st, p3, k1) 3 times, [p1, p1 tbl] in next st, p3, k3, rep from *, end p3.

Row 22 *PS, [p3, k3] 5 times, p3; rep from *, end PS.

Row 23 *[K3, p3] 6 times; rep from *, end k3.

Row 24 *K1, [k1 tbl, k1] in next st, k1, (p3, [sl 2, k1, p2sso]) 5 times, p3; rep from *, end k1, [k1 tbl, k1] in next st, k1.

Row 25 *P4, k23; rep from *, end p4.

Cont in reverse St st until desired length.

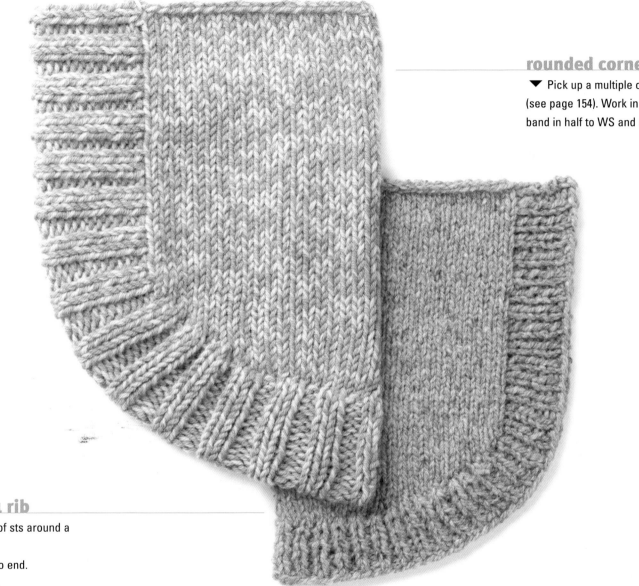

rounded corner/2x2 folded rib

▼ Pick up a multiple of 4 sts around a rounded edge (see page 154). Work in 2x2 rib for 5". Bind off. Fold band in half to WS and sew in place.

rounded corner/1x1 rib

▲▼ Pick up an even number of sts around a rounded edge (see page 154).

Row 1 (WS) *K1, p1; rep from * to end.

Row 2 *P1, k1; rep from * to end.

Rep rows 1 and 2 for 8 rows.

Bind off.

▲ **Colors** A and B

With A, cast on 37 sts
(or a multiple of 10 sts plus 7).

Row 1 (RS) With A, knit.

Row 2 With A, purl.

Row 3 With B, k1, *k5, sl 2 wyib, k1, sl 2 wyib; rep from *, end k6.

Row 4 With B, k1, *k5, sl 2 wyif, k1, sl 2 wyif; rep from *, end k6.

Rows 5 and 6 With A, rep rows 1 and 2.

Row 7 With B, k1, *sl 2 wyib, k1, sl 2 wyib, k5; rep from *, end last rep k1.

Row 8 With B, k1, *sl 2 wyif, k1, sl 2 wyif, k5; rep from *, end last rep k1.

Rep rows 1–8 once more.

Rep rows 1 and 2.

corner

Next row (RS) With B k to last 17 sts, then work row 3 of dots and dashes pat on last 17 sts.

Next row Cont dots and dashes pat on first 17 sts, then with B p to end.

Cont as established in dots and dashes pattern on 17 sts and St st with B on rem sts until desired length.

tuxedo point

▲ **duo angles**

Left point Cast on 2 sts.

Work in St st, inc 1 st at left edge only every RS row until desired point depth, end with a WS row.

Place sts on a holder.

Right point Cast on 2 sts.

Work in St st inc 1 st at right edge only every RS row until same point depth as left point, end with a WS row.

Joining points

Next row (RS) K sts from right point, with same strand of yarn, k sts from left point.

Cont in St st until desired length. Bind off.

cord edge

Work 3-st I-Cord (see page 154) to fit around points.

Sew purchased trim to cord and sew cord to point edges.

stockinette st hearts

▲ Cast on 60 sts (or a multiple of 14 sts plus 4).

2-st LC Sl 1 st to cn and hold to front, k1, then k1 from cn.

2-st RC Sl 1 st to cn and hold to back, k1, then k1 from cn.

RT K2tog leaving sts on LH needle, then k first st again, sl both sts off needle.

LT K 2nd st tbl, then k first st, sl both sts off needle.

Row 1 (WS) Knit.

Row 2 Purl.

Row 3 K8, p2, *k12, p2; rep from *, end k8.

Row 4 P7, 2-st RC, 2-st LC, *p10, 2-st RC, 2-st LC; rep from *, end p7.

Row 5 K7, p4, *k10, p4; rep from *, end k7.

Row 6 P6, 2-st RC, k2, 2-st LC, *p8, 2-st RC, k2, 2-st LC; rep from *, end p6.

Row 7 K6, p6, *k8, p6; rep from *, end k6.

Row 8 P5, 2-st RC, k4, 2-st LC, *p6, 2-st RC, k4, 2-st LC; rep from *, end p5.

Row 9 K5, p8, *k6, p8; rep from *, end k5.

Row 10 P4, *2-st RC, k6, 2-st LC, p4; rep from * to end.

Row 11 K4, *p10, k4; rep from * to end.

Row 12 P4, *k3, RT, LT, k3, p4; rep from * to end.

Row 13 K4, *p4, k2, p4, k4; rep from * to end.

Row 14 P4, *LT, RT, p2, LT, RT, p4; rep from * to end.

Row 15 K5, p2, k4, p2, *k6, p2, k4, p2; rep from *, end k5.

Row 16 P5, M1, k2tog tbl, p4, k2tog, M1, *p6, M1, k2tog tbl, p4, k2tog, M1; rep from *, end p5.

Row 17 Knit.

Row 18 Purl.

corner

Row 1 (WS) K16 sts, p to end.

Row 2 (RS) K to last 16 sts, p16.

Row 3 K8, p2, k6, p to end.

Row 4 K to last 16 sts, p5, 2-st RC, 2-st LC, p7.

Row 5 K7, p4, k5, p to end.

Row 6 K to last 16 sts, p4, 2-st RC, k2, 2-st LC, p6.

Row 7 K6, p6, k4, p to end.

Row 8 K to last 16 sts, p3, 2-st RC, k4, 2-st LC, p5.

Row 9 K5, p8, k3, p to end.

Row 10 K to last 16 sts, p2, 2-st RC, k6, 2-st LC, p4.

Row 11 K4, p10, k2, p to end.

Row 12 K to last 16 sts, p2, k3, RT, LT, k3, p4.

Row 13 K4, p4, k2, p4, k2, p to end.

Row 14 K to last 16 sts, p2, LT, RT, p2, LT, RT, p4.

Row 15 K5, p2, k4, p2, k3, p to end.

Row 16 K to last 16 sts, p3, M1, k2tog tbl, p4, k2tog, M1, p5.

Row 17 K16, p to end.

Row 18 K to last 16 sts, p16.

Rep rows 1–18 until desired length.

tuff cording stitch

▲ **Colors** A and B

With A, cast on 40 sts (or desired number of sts).

Knit 2 rows.

Rows 1 and 3 (RS) With A, knit.

Row 2 With A, k1, p to last st, k1.

Rows 4 to 7 With B, work in St st.

Row 8 (cording row) With A, k1, *wyif, insert needle from the top down into the head of the p st 4 rows below the next st on needle; pick up this loop, place it on LH needle and p it together with next st; rep from * to last st, k1.

Rep rows 1–8 four times.

corner

Next row (RS) Bind off 26 sts, work tuff cording st pat (rows 1–8) to end.

Cont working tuff cording stitch pattern until desired length.

bogus block corner

▲ Cast on 28 sts (or a multiple of 18 sts plus 10).

Knit 1 row.

Rows 1, 3, 5, 7 and 9 (RS) K1, *[sl 1 wyif, p1] 4 times, [k1, p1] 4 times; rep from *, end k1.

Row 2, 4, 6, 8 and 10 P1, *[k1, p1] 4 times, [sl 1 wyib, k1] 4 times; rep from *, end p1.

Rows 11, 13, 15, 17 and 19 K1, *[p1, k1] 4 times, [sl 1 wyif, p1] 4 times; rep from *, end k1.

Rows 12, 14, 16, 18 and 20 P1, *[sl 1 wyib, k1] 4 times, [p1, k1] 4 times; rep from *, end p1.

corner

*Rows 1, 3, 5, 7 and 9 (RS)** K to last 9 sts, [k1, p1] 4 times, end k1.

Rows 2, 4, 6, 8 and 10 P1, [k1, p1] 4 times, p to end.

Rows 11, 13, 15, 17 and 19 K to last 9 sts, [sl 1 wyif, p1] 4 times, end k1.

Rows 12, 14, 16, 18 and 20 P1, [sl 1 wyib, k1] 4 times, p to end.*

Rep from * to * until desired length.

windblown cable

▶ Cast on 17 sts.

4-st LPC SI 2 sts to cn and hold in front, p2, then k2 from cn.

4-st RPC SI 2 sts to cn and hold in back, k2, then p2 from cn.

4-st LC SI 2 sts to cn and hold in front, k2, then k2 from cn.

Row 1 (WS) K1, p1, k2, p4, k4, p2, k2, p1.

Row 2 (RS) K1 tbl, p2, 4-st LPC, p2, k4, p2, k1 tbl, p1.

Row 3 K1, p1, k2, p4, k2, p2, k4, p1.

Row 4 K1 tbl, p4, 4-st LC, 4-st LPC, p2, k1 tbl, p1.

Row 5 K1, p1, k2, p2, k2, p4, k4, p1.

Row 6 K1 tbl, p2, 4-st RPC, 4-st LPC, k2, p2, k1 tbl, p1.

Row 7 K1, p1, k2, p4, k4, p2, k2, p1.

Row 8 K 1tbl, p2, k2, p4, 4-st LC, p2, k1 tbl, p1.

Rep rows 1–8 until desired length. Bind off 14 sts while working row 1. Fasten off.

Unravel 3 sts at right edge for fringe.

Sew on beads.

elf points

▲ ▼ **Colors** A and B

Note Points can be made by incs from the bottom up or decs from the top down in St st.

Bottom up *With A, cast on 1 st. Inc 1 st at beg of every row until desired number of sts for each point. Leave sts on needle. Rep from * for each point. When desired number of points are complete, work across all points and cont in desired pat.

Top down *At edge of piece, mark off desired st width of each point. Working each point separately, dec 1 st at beg of every row until 1 st rem. Fasten off. Rep from * until all points are complete.

With B (angora), make a 3-st I-Cord (see page 154). Sew cord along edge of points making a loop twist at bottom of each point.

& edges

vest point

▲ **Left side** Cast on 2 sts.

Knit 1 row.

*Next row (WS) Cast on 1 st, p to end.

Next row Cast on 2 sts, k to end.*

Rep from * to * until there are 29 sts.

Next row (RS) Cast on 4 sts, k to end.

Next row (WS) Cast on 1 st, p to end.

Rep last 2 rows twice more.

On RS only, inc number of sts needed to complete width of vest front.

Cont as desired.

Right side Work same as left side, reversing shaping.

Ribbing With RS facing, pick up an even amount of sts evenly across lower edge.

Next row (WS) Work in 1x1 rib.

Next row (RS) Rib to st at point, yo, k st at point, yo, rib to end.

Next row Work in established rib.

Rep last 2 rows twice more.

Bind off.

Sew on butterfly buttons.

vintage lattice with cord

▲ Cast on 14 sts.

Row 1 (WS) K2, yo, k2tog, p10.

Row 2 [K first st, sl to LH needle] 3 times, k first st, k2tog, pass first st over 2nd st on RH needle, [yo, k2tog] 3 times, yo, k1, yo, k1 tbl, yo, k2tog, k1.

Rep rows 1 and 2 until desired length, end with pat row 2.

Bind off.

cord

Make a 5-st I-Cord (see page 154) until desired length.

Thread through eyelet row at upper edge.

drop stitch fringe

▲ **First fringe** *Cast on 12 sts (or desired number of sts for edge depth).
Work in St st until desired width.
Next row (RS) K4, drop next 4 sts, cast on 4 sts, k rem 4 sts.
Unravel dropped sts row by row.* Place sts on a spare needle.
Second and third fringes Work same as first fringe from * to *.

Join fringes
Fold one fringe in half to form loop fringe. Pick up sts and work garter st for 1½"/3.75cm. Using 3-needle joining technique (see page 152), add the 2 rem fringes one at a time.

lace corner

▶ Cast on 9 sts.
Row 1 and all RS rows Knit.
Row 2 K3, [k2tog, yo] twice, k1, yo, k1—10 sts.
Row 4 K2, [k2tog, yo] twice, k3, yo, k1—11 sts.
Row 6 K1, [k2tog, yo] twice, k5, yo, k1—12 sts.
Row 8 K3, [yo, k2tog] twice, k1, k2tog, yo, k2tog—11 sts.
Row 10 K4, yo, k2tog, yo, k3tog, yo, k2tog—10 sts.
Row 12 K5, yo, k3tog, yo, k2tog—9 sts.
Rep rows 1–12 until border is required length to corner, end with pat row 6.

corner

Row 1 K10, turn.
Row 2 Sl 1, [yo, k2tog] twice, k1, k2tog, yo, k2tog.
Row 3 K8, turn.
Row 4 Sl 1, yo, k2tog, yo, k3tog, yo, k2tog.
Row 5 K6, turn.
Row 6 Sl 1, yo, k3tog, yo, k2tog.
Row 7 K6, turn.
Row 8 [K2tog, yo] twice, k1, yo, k1.
Row 9 K8, turn.
Row 10 [K2tog, yo] twice, k3, yo, k1.
Row 11 K10, turn.
Row 12 [K2tog, yo] twice, k5, yo, k1.
Row 13 K12.
This completes corner shaping.
Beg with pat row 8, cont in lace corner pattern to next corner, then turn corner. Cont in this manner until border is completed.
Sew on buttons.

& edges

end over end cable fringe

▶ Cast on 20 sts.

Row 1 (WS) P1, k1, p1, k5, p3, k2, p1, k1, p1, pm, p4.

Row 2 (RS) K4, sl marker, k1, p1, k1, p2, k3, p5, k1, p1, k1.

Row 3 P1, k1, p1, k5, p3, k2, p1, k1, p1, sl marker, p4.

Row 4 K4, sl marker, k1, p1, k1, p2, [sl next 6 sts to dpn and hold in front, twist dpn ½ turn clockwise, p3, k3 from dpn], p2, k1, p1, k1.

Rows 5, 7, 9 and 11 P1, k1, p1, k2, p3, k5, p1, k1, p1, sl marker, p4.

Rows 6, 8 and 10 K4, sl marker, k1, p1, k1, p5, k3, p2, k1, p1, k1.

Row 12 K4, sl marker, k1, p1, k1, p2, [sl next 6 sts to dpn and hold in front, twist dpn ½ turn counterclockwise, k3, p3 from dpn], p2, k1, p1, k1.

Rows 13 and 15 P1, k1, p1, k5, p3, k2, p1, k1, p1, sl marker, p4.

Rows 14 and 16 K4, sl marker, k1, p1, k1, p2, k3, p5, k1, p1, k1.

Rep rows 1–16 until desired length. Bind off 16 sts while working row 1. Fasten off. Unravel 4 sts for fringe.

i-cord pods

▶ With dpns, cast on 5 sts.

*Work I-Cord (see page 154) for 1½"/3.75cm as shown or desired length.

pod (worked back and forth in rows)

Inc row (RS) K in front and back of every st—10 sts.

Next row (WS) Purl.

Rep inc row—20 sts.

Cont in St st for 5 rows.

Dec row (RS) [K2tog] to end—10 sts.

Next row (WS) Purl.

Rep dec row—5 sts.*

Rep from * to * until desired length and number of pods.

Stuff pods with fiberfill and sew seams.

Sew to edge of desired piece (shown on rounded edge).

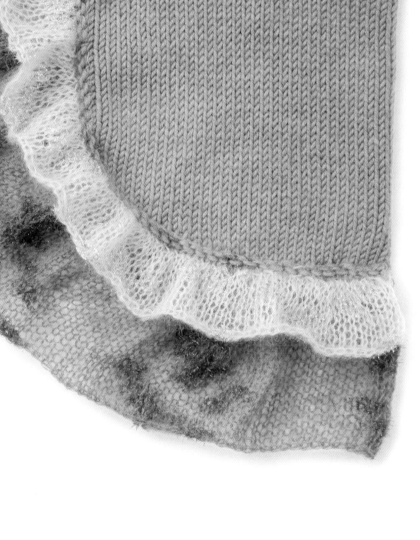

lola's ruffle

▲ **Colors** A and B

First ruffle With A, cast on an even number of sts.

Preparation row K in front and back of every st.

Next row Purl.

Cont in St st for 3½"/7.5cm.

Next row (RS) [K2tog] to end. Place rem sts on a holder.

Second ruffle With B, cast on same amount of sts as first ruffle.

Preparation row K in front and back of every st.

Next row Purl.

Cont in St st for 1½"/4.5cm.

Next row (RS) [K2tog] to end. Place rem sts on a holder.

Joining ruffles

Work sts of both ruffles together, using 3-needle joining technique (see page 152).

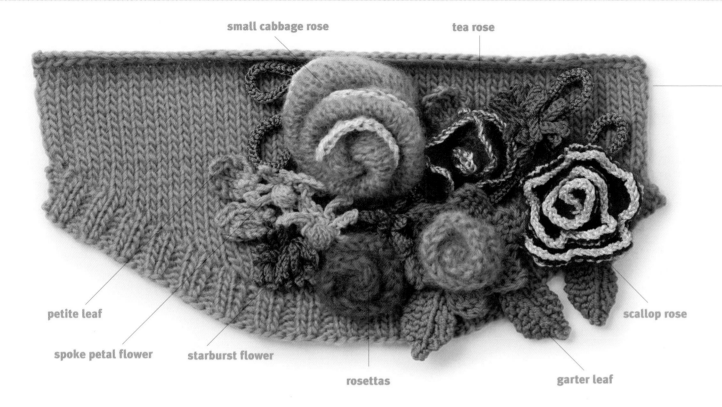

small cabbage rose

tea rose

petite leaf

spoke petal flower

starburst flower

rosettas

garter leaf

scallop rose

english garden edge

Note Florals are sewn to a rounded hem with a picked up 2x2 rib edge.

With yarn choices to correspond with the design, make desired number of each flower, leaf and cord.

Pin and sew in garden cluster to edge of piece.

cord

Make 3-st I-Cords (see page 154) until desired lengths.

garter leaf

Cast on 9 sts.

Rows 1, 3 and 5 (RS) K3, S2KP, k3—7 sts.

Rows 2 and 4 K1, M1, k2, p1, k2, M1, k1—9 sts.

Row 6 K3, p1, k3.

Row 7 K2, S2KP, k2—5 sts.

Row 8 K2, p1, k2.

Row 9 K1, S2KP, k1—3 sts.

Row 10 K1, p1, k1.

Row 11 S2KP—1 st. Fasten off.

petite leaf or bobble

Cast on 1 st.

K in front, back, front, back and front of st—5 sts. P 1 row, k 1 row, p 1 row.

Next row K2tog, k1, k2tog—3 sts.

Next row P3.

Next row SK2P.

For petite leaf, fasten off.

For bobble, fold in half and pull both tails through to WS of finished piece, knot them tog.

spoke petal flower

Note For longer spoke petals, cast on more sts. Use 7 spokes for open flower, 16 for cluster.

Place slip knot on LH needle, *cast on 5 sts, bind off 5 sts, sl rem st back on LH needle, do not turn; rep from * 6 (15) times more. Fasten off. Run threaded tapestry needle through straight edge of piece; pull tightly and secure.

rosette

Cast on 21 sts.

Knit 2 rows.

Pass all sts, one at a time, over first st and fasten off.

Twist to form rosette. Stitch in place.

starburst flower

Cast on 6 sts.

Rows 1, 2 and 3 Knit.

Row 4 Sl 1, k3, with LH needle lift 2nd, 3rd and 4th sts over first st, k2—3 sts.

Row 5 Knit.

Row 6 Cast on 3 sts, k to end—6 sts.

Rep rows 1–6 four times more. Bind off.

Run threaded tapestry needle through straight edge of piece, pulling tightly and secure. Sew final bound-off edge to cast-on edge.

small cabbage rose

Colors A and B

With A, cast on 8 sts.

Row 1 (RS) Knit.

Row 2 and all WS rows Purl.

Rows 3, 5 and 7 *K in front and back of every st—64 sts.

With B, bind off.

Twist to form spiral and shape rose. Stitch in place.

scallop rose

With B, cast on 101 sts. Change to A.

Row 1 (WS) Purl.

Row 2 K2, *k1 and sl back to LH needle, with RH needle lift next 8 sts, one at a time, over this st and off needle, [yo] twice, k first st again, k2; rep from * to end.

Row 3 P1, *p2tog, [k in front, back, front, back and front] of double yo, p1; rep from *, end p1.

Row 4 Knit.

Next row Bind off.

To shape flower, roll bound-off edge to form spiral and stitch in place.

tea rose

With B, cast on 71 sts loosely.

Work in St st for 10 rows. Change to A.

Bind off 4 sts at beg of next 2 rows, then 6 sts at beg of foll 4 rows—39 sts.

Next row (RS) K2tog across row, end k1—20 sts.

Bind off.

With purl side facing, roll bound-off edge to form spiral, and stitch in back shaping rose.

closures

seed stitch flower/2x2 rib band

buttonhole band

▲ Pick up a multiple of 4 sts along right front edge.

Work in 2x2 rib for 3 rows.

Buttonhole row *Rib to buttonhole placement, bind off required number of sts; rep from * across all buttonhole placements, rib to end.

Next row *Rib to within 1 st of the bound-off sts, work into the front and back of this st, then cast on 1 less st than the number of bound-off sts with single cast-on method (see page 152); rep from * across all bound-off sts, rib to end.

Cont in rib for 3 rows. Bind off.

button band

Work same as buttonhole band omitting buttonholes.

Sew on buttons opposite buttonholes.

seed stitch flower

Cast on 30 sts.

Work 6 rows in seed st.

Next row (RS) *Work 5 sts in seed st, then rotate the LH needle 360 degrees counter-clockwise; rep from * to end.

Next row P2tog to end—15 sts.

Next row K2tog to end—8 sts.

Thread tapestry needle with yarn and run through rem sts, gathering them into a circle. Fasten off. Sew around buttonhole.

band with floral embroidery

▲ **cord floral** (using fine mohair yarn)

Work a 3-st I-Cord (see page 154) for needed length. Thread large tapestry needle with cord and work 7 straight sts to form a daisy on desired piece. Sew pearl to center if desired.

daisy with french knots (using dk weight yarn)

Colors A, B and C

With color A, work 7 daisy sts on desired piece.

With color B, work one straight st between each daisy st.

With color C, make one French knot between each daisy st (for embroidery stitch diagrams, see page 153).

basic vertical buttonholes with doughnuts

buttonhole band

▲ Cast on 9 sts, or an uneven number of sts.

Row 1 K1, *p1, k1; rep from * across.

Rep row 1 for seed st to next buttonhole marker.

*Buttonhole row Work in seed st to center st, join
another strand of yarn and bind off 1 st, finish row.
Cont in seed st on both sides for 3 more rows.

Next row Work in seed st to bound-off st, cast on 1 st,
cont with same strand of yarn dropping 2nd strand,
finish row. Cont in seed st to next buttonhole marker.*
Rep from * to * across all buttonhole markers. Cont in
seed st until desired length.

button band

Work same as buttonhole band omitting buttonholes.
Sew buttons opposite buttonholes.

doughnut

Cast on 20 sts loosely.

Work 2 rows in garter st.

Pass all sts, one at a time, over first st and fasten off.

Sew around buttonhole.

open cable

buttonhole band

▲ Cast on 13 sts.

5-st RPC Sl 3 sts to cn and hold to back, k2, sl the p st back to LH needle and p it, then k2 from cn.

3-st LPC Sl 2 sts to cn and hold to front, p1, then k2 from cn.

3-st RPC Sl 1 st to cn and hold to back, k2, then p1 from cn.

Row 1 (WS) P1, k3, p2, k1, p2, k3, p1.

Row 2 Sl 1, p3, 5-st RPC, p3, sl 1.

Row 3 Rep row 1.

Row 4 Sl 1, p2, 3-st RPC, p1, 3-st LPC, p2, sl 1.

Row 5 P1, k2, p2, k3, p2, k2, p1.

Row 6 Sl 1, p1, 3-st RPC, p3, 3-st LPC, p1, sl 1.

Row 7 P1, k1, p2, k5, p2, k1, p1.

Row 8 Sl 1, p1, k2, p1, bind off 3 sts, p1, k2, p1, sl 1.

Row 9 P1, k1, p2, k1, cast on 3 sts, k1, p2, k1, p1.

Row 10 Sl 1, p1, 3-st LPC, p3, 3-st RPC, p1, sl 1.

Row 11 P1, k2, p2, k3, p2, k2, p1.

Row 12 Sl 1, p2, 3-st LPC, p1, 3-st RPC, p2, sl 1.

Rep rows 1–12 until desired length, ending with row 3.

button band

Work as buttonhole band except:

Row 8 Sl 1, p1, k2, p5, k2, p1, sl 1.

Row 9 P1, k1, p2, k5, p2, k1, p1.

Sew buttons opposite buttonholes.

elongated chain cable

buttonhole band

▲ Cast on 14 sts.

4-st LC Sl 2 sts to cn and hold to front, k2, then k2 from cn.

4-st RC Sl 2 sts to cn and hold to back, k2, then k2 from cn.

Rows 1, 3, 5, 9, 11 and 13 (WS) P1, k2, p8, k2, p1.

Row 2 Sl 1, p2, k8, p2, sl 1.

Row 4 Sl 1, p2, 4-st RC, 4-st LC, p2, sl 1.

Row 6 Sl 1, p2, k3, bind off 2 sts, k3, p2, sl 1.

Row 7 P1, k2, p3, cast on 2 sts, p3, k2, p1.

Row 8 Sl 1, p2, k8, p2, sl 1.

Row 10 Sl 1, p2, 4-st LC, 4-st RC, p2, sl 1.

Rows 12 and 14 Sl 1, p2, k8, p2, sl 1.

Rep rows 3–14 for desired length, end work rows 1–3.

button band

Work same as buttonhole band except:

Row 6 (RS) Sl 1, p2, k8, p2, sl 1.

Row 7 P1, k2, p8, k2, p1.

Sew buttons opposite buttonholes.

round cable

buttonhole band

▲ Cast on 14 sts.

Knit 2 rows.

4-st LPC Sl 2 sts to cn and hold to front, p2, then k2 from cn.

4-st RPC Sl 2 sts to cn and hold to back, k2, then p2 from cn.

Row 1 (WS) P1, k4, p4, k4, p1.

Row 2 Sl 1, p4, k4, p4, sl 1.

Row 3 P1, k4, p4, k4, p1.

Row 4 Sl 1, p2, 4-st RPC, 4-st LPC, p2, sl 1.

Row 5 P1, k2, p2, k4, p2, k2, p1.

Row 6 Sl 1, p2, k2, p1, bind off 2 sts, p1, k2, p2, sl 1.

Row 7 P1, k2, p2, k1, cast on 2 sts, k1, p2, k2, p1.

Row 8 Sl 1, p2, k2, p4, k2, p2, sl 1.

Row 9 P1, k2, p2, k4, p2, k2, p1.

Row 10 Sl 1, p2, 4-st LPC, 4-st RPC, p2, sl 1.

Row 11 P1, k4, p4, k4, p1.

Row 12 Sl 1, p4, k4, p4, sl 1.

Rows 13–17 Rep rows 1–5.

Rows 18–21 Rep rows 8 and 9 twice.

Rows 22, 23 and 24 Rep rows 10, 11 and 12.

Rep rows 1–24 for desired length, end by binding off while working row 12.

button band

Work same as buttonhole band except:

Row 6 Sl 1, p2, k2, p4, k2, p2, sl 1.

Row 7 P1, k2, p2, k4, p2, k2, p1.

Sew buttons opposite buttonholes.

carved diamonds

buttonhole band

▲ Cast on 17 sts.

2-st LPC Sl 1 st to cn and hold to front, p1, then k1 from cn.

2-st RPC Sl 1 st to cn and hold to back, k1, then p1 from cn.

Row 1 and all WS rows Purl.

Row 2 K1 tbl, k1, [2-st RPC] 3 times, k1 [2-st LPC] 3 times, k1, k1 tbl.

Row 4 K1 tbl, [2-st RPC] 3 times, k3, [2-st LPC] 3 times, k1 tbl.

Rows 6 and 8 Rep rows 2 and 4.

Row 10 K1 tbl, k6, bind off 3 sts, k to last st, k1 tbl.

Row 11 P7, cast on 3 sts, p7.

Row 12 K1 tbl, [2-st LPC] 3 times, k3, [2-st RPC] 3 times, k1 tbl.

Row 14 K1 tbl, k1, [2-st LPC] 3 times, k1, [2-st RPC] 3 times, k1, k1 tbl.

Rows 16 and 18 Rep rows 12 and 14.

Row 20 K1 tbl, k15, k1 tbl.

Rep rows 1–20 until desired length, end by binding off while working row 15.

button band

Work same as buttonhole band except:

Row 10 K1 tbl, k6, p3, k6, k1 tbl.

Row 11 P7, k3, p7.

Sew buttons opposite buttonholes.

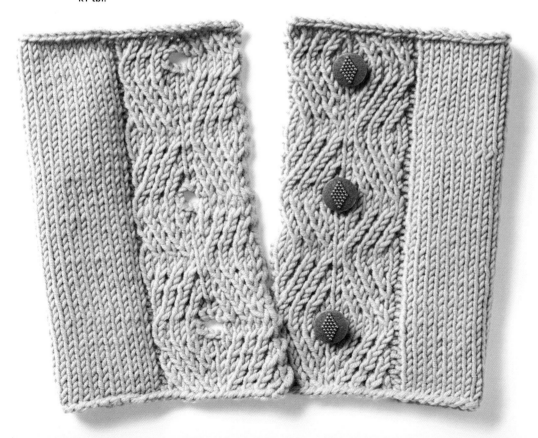

x and o

buttonhole band

▲ Cast on 35 sts.

3-st RC Sl 1 st to cn and hold to back, k2, then k1 from cn.

3-st LC Sl 2 sts to cn and hold to front, k1, then k2 from cn.

1/2 RPC Sl 1 st to cn and hold to back, k2, then p1 from cn.

2/1 LPC Sl 2 sts to cn and hold to front, p1, then k2 from cn.

4-st RC Sl 2 sts to cn and hold to back, k2, then k2 from cn.

4-st LC Sl 2 sts to cn and hold to front, k2, then k2 from cn.

2/2 RPC Sl 2 sts to cn and hold to back, k2, then [p1, k1] from cn.

2/2 LPC Sl 2 sts to cn and hold to front, k1, p1, then k2 from cn.

5-st RC Sl 3 sts to cn and hold to back, k2, then k3 from cn.

5-st LC Sl 2 sts to cn and hold to front, k3, then k2 from cn.

2/3 LPC Sl 2 sts to cn and hold to front, p3, then k2 from cn.

3/2 RPC Sl 3 sts to cn and hold to back, k2, then p3 from cn.

5-st RPC Sl 3 sts to cn and hold to back, k2, then [p1, k2] from cn.

M3 [K1, p1, k1] in next st.

Work 5 tog With yarn at back of work, sl 3, *pass 2nd st on RH needle over first (center) st, sl center st back to LH needle, pass 2nd st on LH needle over*, sl center st back to RH needle; rep from * once more, p center st.

Row 1 (WS) P2, k4, p5, k4, p2, [p18 (facing)].

Row 2 [K17, sl 1], k2, p1, 5-st RC, k1, 5-st LC, p1, k2.

Row 3 P2, k1, p11, k1, p2, [p18].

Row 4 [K17, sl 1], k1, 4-st RC, k7, 4-st LC, k1.

Rows 5, 7, 9, 13 and 15 P17, [p18].

Row 6 [K17, sl 1], 3-st RC, k11, 3-st LC.

Row 8 [K17, sl 1], k17.

Row 10 [K7, bind off 3 sts, k6, sl 1], k7, bind off 3 sts, k6.

Row 11 P7, cast on 3 sts, p7, [p8, cast on 3 sts, p7).

Row 12 [K17, sl 1], k17.

Row 14 [K17, sl 1], 3-st LC, k11, 3-st RC.

Row 16 [K17, sl 1], k1, 2/2 LPC, k7, 2/2 RPC, k1.

Row 17 P2, k1, p11, k1, p2, [p18].

Row 18 [K17, sl 1], k2, p1, 2/3 LPC, k1, 3/2 RPC, p1, k2.

Row 19 P2, k4, p5, k4, p2, [p18].

Row 20 [K17, sl 1], k2, p4, work 5 tog, p4, k2.

Row 21 P2, k9, p2, [p17].

Row 22 [K17, sl 1], k2, p9, k2.

Row 23 P2, k9, p2, [p18].

Row 24 [K17, sl 1], k2, p4, M1, M3, M1, p4, k2.

Row 25 P2, k4, p2, k1, p2, k4, [p18].

Row 26 [K17, sl 1], 2/1 LPC, 3/2 RPC, p1, 2/3 LPC, 1/2 RPC.

Row 27 K1, p4, k7, p4, k1, [p17].

Row 28 [K17, sl 1], p1, 4-st LC, p7, 4-st RC, p1.

Row 29 K1, p4, k7, p4, k1, [p18].

Row 30 [K17, sl 1], 1/2 RPC, 2/1 LPC, p5, 1/2 RPC, 2/1 LPC.

Row 31 P2, k2, p2, k5, p2, k2, p2, [p18]

Row 32 [K17, sl 1], k2, p2, 2/1 LPC, p3, 1/2 RPC, p2, k2.

Row 33 P2, [k3, p2] 3 times, [p18].

Row 34 [K17, sl 1], [k2, p3, 2/1 LPC, p1, 1/2 RPC, p3, k2.

Row 35 P2, k4, p2, k1, p2, k4, p2, [p18].

Row 36 [K17, sl 1], k2, p4, 5-st RPC, p4, p2.

Row 37 P2, k4, p2, k1, p2, k4, p2, [p18].

Row 38 [K17, sl 1], k2, p3, 1/2 RPC, p1, 2/1 LPC, p3, k2.

Row 39 P2, [k3, p2] 3 times, [p18].

Row 40 [K17, sl]1, k2, p2, 1/2 RPC, p3, 2/1 LPC, p2, k2.

Row 41 P2, k2, p2, k5, p2, k2, p2, [p17].

Row 42 [K17[, sl 1], 2/1 LPC, 1/2 RPC, p5, 2/1 LPC, 1/2 RPC.

Row 43 K1, p4, k7, p4, k1, [p18].

Row 44 [K17, sl 1], p1, 4-st RC, p7, 4-st LC, p1.

Row 45 K1, p4, k7, p4, k1, [p18].

Row 46 [K17, sl 1], 1/2 RPC, 2/3 LPC, p1, 3/2 RPC, 2/1 LPC.

Row 47 P2, k4, p2, k1, p2, k4, p2, [p18].

Row 48 [K17, sl 1], k2, p4, work 5 tog, p4, k2.

Row 49 P2, k9, p2, [p18].

Row 50 [K17, sl 1], k2, p9, k2.

Row 51 P2, k9, p2, [p18].

Row 52 [K17, sl 1], k2, p4, M1, M3, M1, p4, k2.

Rep rows 1–52 until desired length, end by binding off while working row 21.

(Sample shows buttons sewn to a ribbed band.)

leaf frog

▶ Work two 3-st I-Cords (see page 154), 7½"/19cm for button, and 6"/15cm for loop. Inc 2 sts on last row—5 sts. Do not bind off. Work leaf as follows:

leaf

Row 1 (RS) K2, yo, k1, yo, k2—7 sts.

Row 2 and all WS rows Purl.

Row 3 K3, yo, k1, yo, k3—9 sts.

Row 5 Ssk, k5, k2tog—7 sts.

Row 7 Ssk, k3, k2tog—5 sts.

Row 9 Ssk, k1, k2tog—3 sts.

Row 10 S2KP. Fasten off.

Pick up 3 sts of I-Cord cast-on edge, inc 2 sts—5 sts, work leaf.

Fold 6"/15cm cord in half, twist forming a button loop, pin and stitch the leaves and cord in place (see photo). Secure loop to piece. Work in same way for 7½"/19cm cord, but make a knot at the end instead of a loop. The knot forms the button. Secure the button. Sew hook and eye under frogs for more secure closure.

slotted cable panel

buttonhole band

▲ Cast on 18 sts.

4-st RPC Sl 2 sts to cn and hold to back, k2, then p2 from cn.

4-st LPC Sl 2 sts to cn and hold to front, p2, then k2 from cn.

Preparation rows

(WS) K1, p1, k4, p6, k4, p1, k1.

(RS) P1, k1, p4, k6, p4, k1, p1.

Row 1 (WS) K1, p1, k4, p2, [yo] twice, bind off 2 sts, p2, k4, p1, k1.

Row 2 P1, k1, p4, k2, [k1, k1 tbl] in double yo, k2, p4, k1, p1.

Row 3 K1, p1, k4, p6, k4, p1, k1.

Row 4 P1, k1, p2, 4-st RPC, k2, 4-st LPC p2, k1, p1.

Rows 5, 7, 9 and 11 K1, p1, [k2, p2] 3 times, k2, p1, k1.

Rows 6, 8, and 10 P1, k1, [p2, k2] 3 times, p2, k1, p1.

Row 12 P1, k1, p2, 4-st LPC, k2, 4-st RPC, p2, k1, p1.

Row 13 K1, p1, k4, p6, k4, p1, k1.

Row 14 P1, k1, p4, k6, p4, k1, p1.

Rep rows 1–14 until desired length, end by binding off while working pat row 3.

button band

Work same as buttonhole band except:

Row 1 K1, p1, k4, p6, k4, p1, k1.

Row 2 P1, k1, p4, k6, p4, k1, p1.

Sew buttons opposite buttonholes.

chain cable

buttonhole band

▲ Cast on 18 sts.

4-st RC Sl 2 sts to cn and hold to back, k2, then k2 from cn.

4-st LC Sl 2 sts to cn and hold to front, k2, then k2 from cn.

Rows 1, 3, 5 and 7 (WS) P1, k1, p1, k2, p8, k2, p1, k1, p1.

Row 2 K1, p1, k1, p2, 4-st RC, 4-st LC, p2, k1, p1, k1.

Row 4 K1, p1, k1, p2, k3, yo, k2tog, k3, p2, k1, p1, k1.

Row 6 K1, p1, k1, p2, 4-st LC, 4-st RC, p2, k1, p1, k1.

Row 8 K1, p1, k1, p2, k8, p2, k1, p1, k1.

Rep rows 1–8 for desired length, end by binding off while working row 8.

button band

Work same as buttonhole band except:

Row 4 K1, p1, k1, p2, k8, p2, k1, p1, k1.

Sew buttons opposite buttonholes.

woven check

buttonhole band

▲ Cast on 35 sts.

Rows 1 and 3 (RS) [K17 (facing), sl 1], k1, sl 3 wyif, k9, sl 3 wyif, k1.

Rows 2 and 4 Purl.

Row 5 [K7, bind off 3 sts, k6, sl 1], k1, sl 3 wyif, k3, bind off 3 sts, k2, sl 3 wyif, k1.

Row 6 P7, cast on 3 sts, p7, [p8, cast on 3 sts, p7].

Rows 7 and 9 [K17, sl 1], k1, sl 3 wyif, k9, sl 3 wyif, k1.

Rows 8, 10, 12 and 14 Purl.

Rows 11, 13 and 15 [K 17, sl 1], k1, [sl 3 wyif] 4 times, k1.

Row 16 Purl.

Rep rows 1–16 until desired length, end by binding off while working row 10.

button band

Work same as buttonhole band except:

Row 5 [K17, sl 1], sl 3 wyif, k9, sl 3 wyif, k1.

Row 6 Purl.

Sew buttons opposite buttonholes.

bobble diamonds

MB (Make bobble) (see page 152)

buttonhole band

▲ Cast on 19 sts.

Preparation row Knit.

Row 1 (RS) [P1, k1] 4 times, p1, MB, [p1, k1] 4 times, p1.

Row 2 and all WS rows *K1, p1; rep from *, end k1.

Rows 3, 7 and 11 *P1, k1; rep from *, end p1.

Row 5 [P1, k1] 3 times, p1, MB, p1, k1, p1, MB, [p1, k1] 3 times, p1.

Rows 9 and 17 [P1, k1], p1, MB, [p1, k1] 3 times, p1, MB, [p1, k1] twice, p1.

Row 13 P1, k1, p1, MB, [p1, k1] twice, make a 3-st one row buttonhole (see page 154), [k1, p1] twice, MB, p1, k1, p1.

Rows 15, 19 and 23 *P1, k1; rep from *, end p1.

Row 21 [P1, k1] 3 times, p1, MB, p1, k1, p1, MB, [p1, k1] 3 times, p1.

Row 24 *K1, p1; rep from *, end k1.

Rep rows 1–24 until desired length, end by binding off while working row 2.

button band

Cast on 19 sts. Work in 1x1 rib until desired length. Bind off. Sew buttons opposite buttonholes.

M5 K in front, back, front, back and front of next st.

M4 K in front, back, front and back of next st.

M3 K in front, back and front of next st.

2-st LPC Sl 1 st to cn and hold to front, p1, then k1 from cn.

2-st RPC Sl 1 st to cn and hold to back, k1, then p1 from cn.

3-st LC Sl 1 st to cn and hold to front, k2, then k1 from cn.

hidden button band

button band

▲ Cast on 26 sts.

Preparation row Knit.

Rows 1 and 3 (RS) [K11 (facing), sl 1], p13, sl 1.

Rows 2 and 4 P1, k13, [p12].

Row 3 Rep row 1.

Row 5 [K11, sl 1], p6, M5, p6, sl 1.

Row 6 P1, k6, p5, k6, [p12].

Row 7 [K11, sl 1], p6, k5, p6, sl 1.

Row 8 P1, k6, p5, k6, [p12].

Row 9 [K11, sl 1], p2, M5, p3, ssk, k1, k2tog, p3, M5, p2, sl 1.

Row 10 P1, k2, p5, k3, p3tog, k3, p5, k2, [p12].

Row 11 [K11, sl 1], p2, k5, p3, k1 tbl, p3, k5, p2, sl 1.

Row 12 P1, k2, p5, k3, p1, k3, p5, k2, [p12].

Row 13 [K11, sl 1], p2, ssk, k1, k2tog, p3, k1, p3, ssk, k1, k2tog, p2, sl 1.

Row 14 P1, k2, p3tog, k3, p1, k3, p3tog, k2, [p12].

Row 15 [K11, sl 1], p2, k1 tbl, p3, k1, p3, k1 tbl, p2, sl 1.

Row 16 P1, k2, [p1, k3] twice, p1, k2, [p12].

Row 17 [K11, sl 1], p2, 2-st LPC, p2, k1, p2, 2-st RPC, p2, sl 1.

Row 18 P1, k3, [p1, k2] twice, p1, k3, [p12].

Row 19 [K11, sl 1], p3, 2-st LPC, p1, k1, p1, 2-st RPC, p3, sl 1.

Row 20 P1, k4, [p1, k1] twice, p1, k4, [p12].

Row 21 [K11, sl 1], p4, 2-st LPC, k1, 2-st RPC, p4, sl 1.

Row 22 P1, k5, p3, k5, [p12].

Row 23 [K11, sl 1], p2, M4, p2, 3-st LC, p2, M4, p2, sl 1.

Row 24 P1, k2, p4, k2, p3, k2, p4, k2, [p12].

Row 25 [K11, sl 1], p2, k4, p2, k3, p2, k4, p2, sl 1.

Row 26 P1, k2, p4, k2, p3, k2, p4, k2, [p12].

Row 27 [K11, sl 1], p2, k4tog, p2, 3-st LC, p2, k4tog, p2, sl 1.

Row 28 P1, k5, p3, k5, p1, p11.

Row 29 K11, sl 1, p4, 2-st RPC, k1, 2-st LPC, p4, sl 1.

Row 30 P1, k4, [p1, k1] twice, p1, k4, [p12].

Row 31 [K11, sl 1], p3, 2-st RPC, p1, k1, p1, 2-st LPC, p3, sl 1.

Row 32 P1, k3, [p1, k2] twice, p1, k3, [p12].

Row 33 [K11, sl 1], p2, 2-st RPC, p2, k1, p2, 2-st LPC, p2, sl 1.

Row 34 P1, k2, [p1, k3] twice, p1, k2, [p12].

Row 35 [K11, sl 1], p2, M3, p3, k1, p3, M3, p2, sl 1.

Row 36 P1, k2, p3, k3, p1, k3, p3, k2, [p12].

Row 37 [K11, sl 1], p2, [k1, M1] twice, k1, p3, k1, p3, [k1, M1] twice, k1, p2, sl 1.

Row 38 P1, k2, p5, k3, p1, k3, p5, k2, [p12].

Row 39 [K11, sl 1], p2, k5, p3, M3, p3, k5, p2, sl 1.

Row 40 P1, k2, p5tog, k3, p3, k3, p5tog, k2, [p12].

Row 41 [K11, sl 1], p6, [k1, M1] twice, k1, p6, sl 1.

Row 42 P1, k6, p5, k6, [p12].

Row 43 [K11, sl 1], p6, k5, p6, sl 1.

Row 44 P1, k6, p5tog, k6, [p12].

Rows 45 and 47 [K11, sl 1], p13, sl 1.

Rows 46 and 48 P1, k13, [p12].

Rep rows 1–48 until desired length.

Fold facing to WS and sew in place. Sew buttons to facing behind center of motif.

buttonhole band

Cast on 11 sts. Work in St st, placing buttonholes opposite buttons.

crossed garter points

button band

▶ Pick up a multiple of 15 sts along right front edge.

First point *Working on next 15 sts only, knit 2 rows.

Dec 1 st at beg of every row until 1 st rem. Fasten off.*

Rep from * to * to end.

buttonhole band

Work same as button band, placing 2-st buttonhole

(see page 154) on 5th row center of each point.

Sew buttons opposite buttonholes.

guinivere's closure

▶ Make a 3-st I-Cord (see page 154)

15"/38cm long. Fasten off. Follow diagram to

shape cord leaving a loop at tip of closure for

button loop, sew cord in position on desired

piece (see page 154).

Sew button opposite button loop.

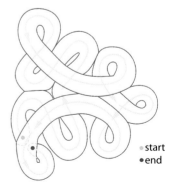

• start
• end

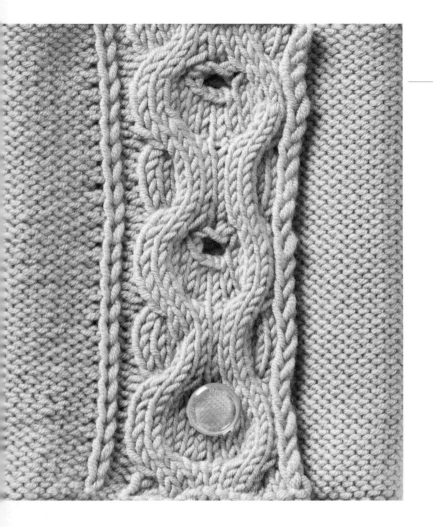

medallion panel cable

buttonhole band

▲ Cast on 17 sts.

6-st LC Sl 3 sts to cn and hold to front, k3, then k3 from cn.

6-st RC Sl 3 sts to cn and hold to back, k3, then k3 from cn.

Rows 1 and 3 (RS) P2, k13, p2.

Rows 2 and 4 K2, p13, k2.

Row 5 P2, 6-st RC, k1, 6-st LC, p2.

Rows 6 and 8 K2, p13, k2.

Rows 7 and 11 P2, k13, p2.

Row 9 P2, k5, bind off 3 sts, k4, p2.

Row 10 K2, p5, cast on 3 sts, p5, k2.

Row 12 K2, p13, k2.

Row 13 P2, 6-st LC, k1, 6-st RC, k2.

Row 14 K2, p13, k2.

Row 15 P2, k13, p2.

Row 16 K2, p13, k2.

Rep rows 1–16 until desired length.

button band

Work same as buttonhole band except:

Row 9 P2, k13, p2.

Row 10 K2, p13, k2.

Sew buttons opposite buttonholes.

single cable twist

button band

▶ With RS facing, pick up a multiple of 8 sts plus 2 along front edge.

6-st LC Sl 3 sts to cn and hold to front, k3, then k 3 from cn.

Row 1 (WS) *K2, p6; rep from *, end k2.

Row 2 *P2, k6; rep from *, end p2.

Row 3 *K2, p6; rep from *, end k2.

Row 4 *P2, 6-st LC; rep from *, end p2.

Row 5 *K2, p6; rep from *, end k2.

Bind off.

buttonhole band

Work same as button band working buttonholes on rows 2 and 3 as follows:

Row 2 *P2, k6, bind off 2 sts, k5; rep from *, end p2.

Row 3 *K2, p6, cast on 2 sts, p6; rep from *, end p2.

Sew buttons opposite buttonholes.

galway frog

▶ Make two 3-st I-Cords (see page 154) 13.5"/34.5cm and 15"/38cm for frog with loop. Fasten off. Follow diagram to shape cord, leaving a loop at end of one frog for button loop. Sew cords in position on desired piece (see page 154).

Sew button on frog opposite button loop.

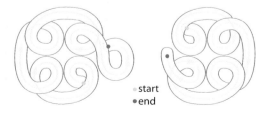

• start
• end

ball and chain

chain

▶ With dpns, cast on 5 sts.

Row 1 K1, [p1, k1] twice, do not turn, slide sts to other end of needle.

Row 2 P1, [k1, p1] twice, do not turn, slide sts to other end of needle.

Rep rows 1 and 2 for seed st cord for 7½"/19cm. Sew ends tog. Twist cord 3 times. Sew twist in place leaving a loop at each end.

Sew to desired piece.

ball buttons

Cast on 9 sts, leaving a long tail for seaming.

Row 1 K in front and back of every st—18 sts.

Row 2 and all WS rows Purl.

Rows 3, 5 and 7 Knit.

Row 9 K2tog to end—9 sts.

With tapestry needle run tail through 9 sts, gather and secure. Thread cast-on tail and run through cast-on sts, gather and secure. Stuff with fiberfill and sew side edges tog. Attach ball buttons opposite chain loops.

raised leaf

button band

▲ Cast on 11 sts.

M3 [K1, p1, k1] in next st.

Row 1 (RS) P1, k1, p3, M3, p3, k1, p1.

Row 2 K1, p1, k3, p3, k3, p1, k1.

Row 3 P1, k1, p3, k1, M1, k1, M1, k1, p3, k1, p1.

Row 4 K1, p1, k3, p5, k3, p1, k1.

Row 5 P1, k1, p3, k2, M1, k1, M1, k2, p3, k1, p1.

Row 6 K1, p1, k3, p7, k3, p1, k1.

Row 7 P1, k1, p3, k3, M1, k1, M1, k3, p3, k1, p1.

Row 8 K1, p1, k3, p9, k3, p1, k1.

Row 9 P1, k1, p3, ssk, k5, k2tog, p3, k1, p1.

Row 10 K1, p1, k3, p7, k3, p1, k1.

Row 11 P1, k1, p3, ssk, k3, k2tog, p3, k1, p1.

Row 12 K1, p1, k3, p5, k3, p1, k1.

Row 13 P1, k1, p3, ssk, k1, k2tog, p3, k1, p1.

Row 14 K1, p1, k3, p3, k3, p1, k1.

Row 15 P1, k1, p3, SK2P, p3, k1, p1.

Row 16 K1, p1, k3, p1, k3, p1, k1.

Row 17 P1, k1, p3, k1 tbl, p3, k1, p1.

Row 18 K1, p1, k3, p1, k3, p1, k1.

Row 19 P1, k1, p3, k1 tbl, p3, k1, p1.

Row 20 K1, p1, k3, p1, k3, p1, k1.

Rep rows 1–20 until desired length, end by binding off while working row 16.

buttonhole band

Work same as button band using eyelet on row 13 for buttonholes.

Sew buttons opposite buttonholes.

bulky double cable

buttonhole band

▲ Cast on 18 sts.

6-st RC Sl 3 sts to cn and hold in back, k3, then k3 from cn.

6-st LC Sl 3 sts to cn and hold in front, k3, then k3 from cn.

Rows 1, 3, 5 and 9 (WS) P1, k2, p12, k2, p1.

Row 2 Sl 1, p2, 6-st RC, 6-st LC, p2, sl 1.

Rows 4, 8 and 10 Sl 1, p2, k12, p2, sl 1.

Row 6 Sl 1, p2, k4, bind off 4 sts, k3, p2, sl 1.

Row 7 P1, k2, p4, cast on 4 sts, p4, k2, sl 1.

Rep rows 1–10 until desired length, end by binding off while working row 10.

button band

Work same as buttonhole band except:

Row 6 Sl 1, p2, k12, p2, sl 1.

Row 7 P1, k2, p12, k2, p1.

Sew buttons opposite buttonholes.

horseshoe cable

buttonhole band

▲ Cast on 14 sts.

4-st RC Sl 2 sts to cn and hold to back, k2, then k2 from cn.

4-st LC Sl 2 to cn and hold to front, k2, then k2 from cn.

Rows 1 and 3 P1, k2, p8, k2.

Rows 2 and 10 Sl 1, p2, 4-st RC, 4-st LC, p2, sl 1.

Row 4 Sl 1, p2, k3, bind off 2 sts, k2, p2, sl 1.

Row 5 P1, k2, p3, cast on 2 sts, p3, k2, p1.

Rows 6, 8, 12 and 14 Sl 1, p2, k8, p2, sl 1.

Rows 7, 9, 11, 13 and 15 Rep row 1.

Row 16 Sl 1, p2, k8, p2, sl 1.

Rep rows 1–16 until desired length, end by binding off while working row 8.

button band

Work same as buttonhole band except:

Row 4 Sl 1, p2, k8, p2, sl 1.

Row 5 P1, k2, p8, k2, p1.

Sew buttons opposite buttonholes.

vertical 1x1 rib band

button band

▲ Cast on 11 sts.

Row 1 (RS) K1, *p1, k1; rep from * to end.

Row 2 P1, *k1, p1; rep from * to end.

Rep rows 1 and 2 until desired length. Bind off. Sew band to front edge.

buttonhole band

Work same as button band except working 2-st buttonholes (see page 154) evenly spaced as desired.

Sew beads along edge and buttons opposite buttonholes.

victorian boot button loops

buttonhole band

▲ ▶ Beg with a multiple of 10 sts plus 2 (and end with a multiple of 6 sts plus 2).

Row 1 (WS) Purl.

Row 2 K2, *k1 and sl back to LH needle, lift next 7 sts, one at a time, over this st and off the needle, [yo] twice, k the first st again, k2, rep from * to end.

Row 3 P1, *p2tog, [k1, p1] twice in double yo, p1, rep from *, end k1.

Row 4 Knit.

Row 5 Purl.

Cont as desired for a wider band or bind off and sew to edge.

(Sample shows victorian boot button loops over a 1x1 rib button band.)

Sew buttons opposite loops.

ribbed tab/cord button

button loop

▶ With dpns, invisibly cast on 3 sts (see page 152). Work I-Cord (see page 152) for 2½"/7.5cm or desired length.

tab

With 3 sts on needle, pick up 3 sts from provisional cast-on and cast on 3 sts. Work in 1x1 rib across all 9 sts, cast on 3 sts—12 sts. Cont in rib for 1½"/3.75cm. Bind off. Sew tab to edge of desired piece.

Make cord button (see page 154) and sew opposite tab.

doughnut frog

doughnut

▶ Cast on 20 sts. Knit 2 rows.

Pass all sts, one at a time, over first st and fasten off.

doughnut frog

Work 3 doughnuts and sew together to form frog (see photo). Work 3-st I-Cord (see page 154) until desired length for button loop and sew to frog. Sew frog to desired piece.

Make a cord button (see page 154) and sew opposite frog.

pretzel frog

▶ Work a 3-st I-Cord (see page 154) 15"/38cm in length. Fasten off. Follow diagram to shape cord, leaving a loop at end of frog for button loop. Sew cord in position on desired piece (see page 154).

Make a cord button (see page 154).

Sew button opposite button loop.

start
end

seed stitch blind band

button band

▲ Cast on 19 sts (or an odd number of sts). Work in seed st until desired length. Bind off.

buttonhole band

Work same as button band until desired length, working 3-row vertical buttonholes (see page 154) 5 sts from front edge and evenly spaced along buttonhole band.

Sew buttons to wrong side of button band opposite buttonholes.

flower

Place a slip knot on needle.

*Cast on 7 sts using single cast-on (see page 152), bind off 7 sts, sl rem st back on LH needle, do not turn; rep from * 7 times more. Fasten off. Run threaded tapestry needle through straight edge of piece. Pull tightly and secure. Sew flower to RS of button band opposite buttons.

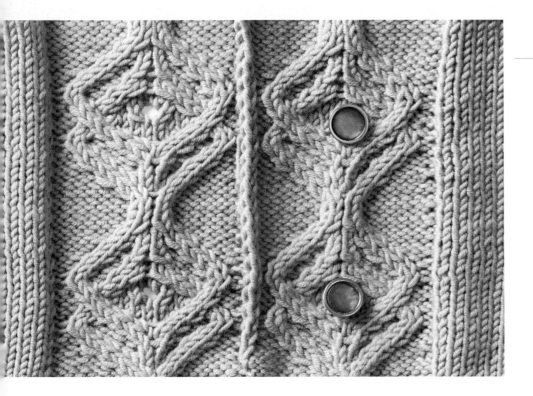

2/2 **LPC** Sl 2 sts to cn and hold to front, [k1, p1], then k2 from cn.

2/2 **RPC** Sl 2 sts to cn and hold to back, k2, then [p1, k1] from cn.

4-st **LPC** Sl 2 sts to cn and hold to front, p2, then k2 from cn.

4-st **RPC** Sl 2 sts to cn and hold in back, k2, then p2 from cn.

1/1 **LC** Sl 1 st to cn and hold to front, k1, then k1 from cn.

1/1 **RC** Sl 1 st to cn and hold to back, k1, then k1 from cn.

4-st **LC** Sl 2 sts to cn and hold to front, k2, then k2 from cn.

4-st **RC** Sl 2 sts to cn and hold to back, k2, then k2 from cn.

1/1 **LPC** Sl 1 st to cn and hold to front, p1, then k1 from cn.

1/1 **RPC** Sl 1 st to cn and hold to back, k1, then p1 from cn.

double entendre

buttonhole band

▲ Cast on 24 sts.

Preparation row (WS) Sl 1, k9, p4, k10.

Row 1 (RS) Sl 1, p7, 2/2 RPC, 2/2 LPC, p8.

Row 2 Sl 1, k7, [p2, k1] twice, p2, k8.

Row 3 Sl 1, p5, 4-st RPC, p1, k2, p1, 4-st LPC, p6.

Row 4 Sl 1, k5, [p2, k3] twice, p2, k6.

Row 5 Sl 1, p3, 4-st RPC, p2, 1/1 RC, 1/1 LC, p2, 4-st LPC, p4.

Row 6 Sl 1, k3, p2, k4, p4, k4, p2, k4.

Row 7 Sl 1, p1, 4-st RPC, p2, 4-st RC, 4-st FC, p2, 4-st LPC, p2.

Row 8 Sl 1, k1, p2, k4, p8, k4, p2, k2.

Row 9 Sl 1, p1, 4-st LPC, 4-st RC, k4, 4-st LC, 4-st RPC, p2.

Row 10 Sl 1, k3, p16, k4.

Row 11 Sl 1, p3, 4-st RC, k2, k2tog, [yo] twice, k2tog, k2, 4-st LC, p4.

Row 12 Sl 1, k3, p7, [p1, p1 tbl] in double yo, p7, k4.

Row 13 Sl 1, p1, 4-st RPC, 4-st LPC, k4, 4-st RPC, 4-st LPC, p2.

Row 14 Sl 1, k1, p2, k4, p8, k4, p2, k2.

Row 15 Sl 1, p1, 4-st LPC, p2, 4-st LPC, 4-st RPC, p2, 4-st RPC, p2.

Row 16 Sl 1, k3, p2, k4, p4, k4, p2, k4.

Row 17 Sl 1, p3, 4-st LPC, p2, 1/1 LPC, 1/1 RPC, p2, 4-st RPC, p4.

Row 18 Sl 1, k5, [p2, k3] twice, p2, k6.

Row 19 Sl 1, p5, 4-st LPC, p1, k2, p1, 4-st RPC, p6.

Row 20 Sl 1, k7, [p2, k1] twice, p2, k8.

Row 21 Sl 1, p7, 4-st LPC, 4-st RPC, p8.

Row 22 Sl 1, k9, p4, k10.

Row 23 Sl 1, p9, k4, p10.

Row 24 Sl 1, k9, p4, k10.

Rep rows 1–24 for desired length, end by binding off while working row 22.

button band

Work same as buttonhole band except:

Row 11 Sl 1, p3, 4-st RC, k8, 4-st LC, p4.

Row 12 Sl 1, k3, p16, k4.

Sew buttons opposite buttonholes.

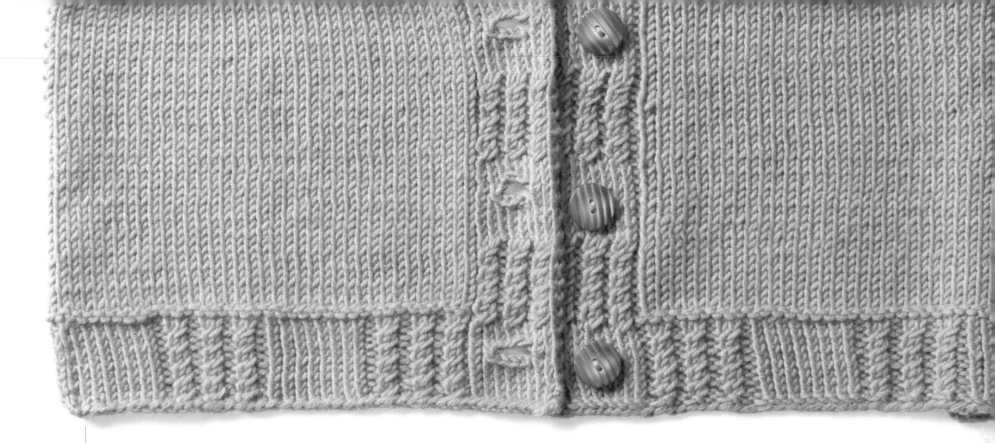

bavarian check corner/buttonholes

border

▲ Cast on a multiple of 18 sts plus 10.

Work rows 1–10 of Bavarian check pattern.

buttonhole band

Next row (RS) Cont with row 11 of Bavarian check pat on first 10 sts, then p rem sts.

Next row P to last 10 sts, then cont Bavarian check pat to end.

Cont as established in Bavarian check pattern on 10 sts and St st on rem sts for desired length.

button band

Work same as buttonhole band except:

Row 5 P1, k8 tbl, *[p1, RT] 3 times, p1, k8 tbl; rep from *, end p1.

Row 6 K1, *p8 tbl, [k1, p2] 3 times, k1; rep from *, end last rep p8 tbl, k1.

Sew buttons opposite buttonholes.

bavarian check pattern

(multiple of 18 sts plus 10)

RT K 2nd st on LH needle, k first st on LH needle, slip both sts from needle tog.

Rows 1, 3, 7 and 9 (RS) P1, *k8 tbl, [p1, RT] 3 times, p1; rep from *, end k8 tbl, p1.

Rows 2, 4, 8 and 10 K1, *p8 tbl, [k1, p2] 3 times, k1; rep from *, end p8 tbl, k1.

Row 5 P1, k3 tbl, bind off 2 sts, k2 tbl, *[p1, RT] 3 times, p1, k8 tbl; rep from *, end p1.

Row 6 K1, *p8 tbl, [k1, p2] 3 times, k1; rep from * to last 9 sts, p3 tbl, cast on 2 sts, p3 tbl, k1.

Rows 11, 13, 15, 17 and 19 *[P1, RT] 3 times, p1, k8 tbl; rep from *, end last rep [p1, RT] 3 times, p1.

Rows 12, 14, 16, 18 and 20 *[K1, p2] 3 times, k1, p8 tbl; rep from *, end last rep [k1, p2] 3 times, k1.

BELLE EPOQUE JACKET

SIZES

To fit Small (Medium, Large). Directions are for smallest size with larger sizes in parentheses. If there is only one figure, it applies to all sizes.

KNITTED MEASUREMENTS

- Bust 36 (40, 44)"/91.5 (101.5, 111.5)cm
- Length 20 (20½, 21)"/51 (52, 53.5)cm
- Upper arm 13¼ (14¼, 15½)"/33.5 (36, 39.5)cm

MATERIALS

- 9 (10, 11) 1¾oz/50g balls (each approx 120yd/ 110m) of GGH/Muench Yarns Maxima (100% extra fine superwash merino wool) in #5 chocolate (MC) (3)
- 1 ball each in #32 pumpkin (A), #18 cinnamon (B), #8 taupe (C), #13 sage (D) and #9 army green (E)
- One pair size 5 (3.75mm) needles OR SIZE TO OBTAIN GAUGE
- 2 size 5 (3.75mm) double-pointed needles
- Stitch holders
- Tapestry needle
- Beads #17056 from Bead Warehouse

GAUGES

- 21 sts and 28 rows = 4"/10cm over St st.
- 26 sts and 28 rows = 4"/10cm over Pat 1.

TAKE TIME TO CHECK GAUGES.

PATTERN 1

(multiple of 4 sts plus 2)

Row 1 (RS) *K1, p1; rep from * to end.
Row 2 *K3, p1; rep from *, end k2.
Row 3 P2, *k1, p3; rep from * to end.
Row 4 Rep row 1.
Row 5 *K1, p3; rep from *, end k2.
Row 6 K1, p1, *k3, p1; rep from * to end.
Rep rows 1 to 6 for Pat 1.

PATTERN 2—PICOT HEM

(multiple of 2 sts plus 1)

This edging may be used on cast-on or bind-off edge.

Rows 1–4 Beg with a RS row, work in St st.
Row 5 (Picot) K1, *yo, k2tog; rep from * to end.
Rows 6–8 Work in St st.

BACK

With MC, cast on 99 (111, 123) sts. Work rows 1–8 of Pat 2 picot hem.

Next row (RS) K, inc 19 sts evenly spaced across row—118 (130, 142) sts. P 1 row. Work in Pat 1 for 11"/28cm, end with a WS row.

Armhole shaping

Bind off 5 sts at beg of next 2 rows, 2 sts at beg of next 2 rows. Dec 1 st each side every other row twice—100 (112, 124) sts. Work even until armhole measures 8 (8½, 9)"/20.5 (21.5, 23)cm, end with a WS row. K 35 (41, 47) sts and place on a holder for shoulder, bind off center 30 sts, k rem sts and place on a holder.

LEFT FRONT

With MC, cast on 47 (55, 63) sts. Work rows 1–8 of Pat 2 picot hem.

Next row (RS) K, inc 11 sts evenly spaced across row—58 (66, 74) sts. P1 row. Work Pat 1 for 11"/28cm, ending with pat row 4.

Armhole shaping

Shape armhole at side edge as for back, end with a RS row—49 (57, 65) sts.

Neck shaping

Bind off 1 st at neck edge (beg of WS row) on next row, then every other row 1 (3, 5) times, then every 4th row 12 times—35 (41, 47) sts. Work even until same length as back to shoulder. Place sts on a holder.

RIGHT FRONT

Work to correspond to left front, reversing all shaping.

SLEEVES

With MC, cast on 53 (61, 69) sts. Work rows 1–8 of Pat 2 picot hem.

Next row (RS) K, inc 9 sts evenly spaced across row—62 (70, 78) sts. P1 row. Work Pat 1, inc 1 st each side every 6th row 12 times—86 (94, 102) sts. Work even until piece measures 12"/30.5cm above picot row, end with a WS row.

Cap shaping

Bind off 5 sts at beg of next 2 rows, 3 sts at beg of next 2 rows. Dec 1 st each side every other row 14 (16, 18) times. Bind off 3 sts at beg of next 6 rows, then 5 (6, 7) sts at beg of next 2 rows. Bind off rem 14 (16, 18) sts.

LEFT COLLAR

With MC, cast on 3 sts. Working in St st, inc 1 st at beg of every RS row 21 times, then at beg of every other RS row 11 times—35 sts. Work even until piece measures 12½(13, 13½)"/31.5 (33, 34.2)cm or until it reaches from beg of front neck shaping to center back of neck. Place sts on a holder.

RIGHT COLLAR

Work as for left collar, but work incs at end of RS rows. Place sts on a separate holder.

BACK PEPLUM

With MC, cast on 111 (121, 131) sts. Work in St st for 5 rows. K next row on WS for turning ridge. Cont in St st for 4½"/11.5cm. Bind off.

FRONT PEPLUMS (make 2)

With MC, cast on 55 (63, 71) sts. Work in St st for 5 rows. K next row on WS for turning row. Cont in St st for 4½"/11.5cm. Bind off.

CUFFS (make 2)

With MC, cast on 80 sts. Work in St st for 5 rows. K next row on WS for turning row. Cont in St st for 9½"/24cm. Bind off.

FINISHING

Block collar, cuffs and peplum pieces.

Embroidery

Following charts 1–3, duplicate st patterns on collar, cuff and peplum pieces, then add straight-stitch details.

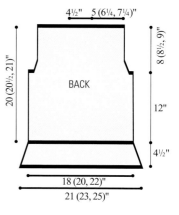

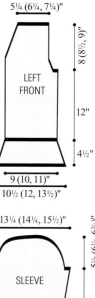

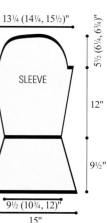

Note *When reading chart, begin with stitch 1 and read from right to left. If the piece has more sts than shown on the chart, work to end of chart then begin with stitch 1 again.* Add beads, as desired, to flower centers. Join shoulder seams using 3-needle bind-off technique (see page 152). Turn all hems to WS along picot row and sew in place. Set in sleeves. Sew side and sleeve seams. Sew cuff seam. Fold cuff hem along turning ridge and sew in place. Sew cuffs to bottom edge of sleeves under picot hem easing in fullness at top of cuff.

Fold hems along turning ridges on back and front peplums and sew in place. Sew back and front peplums under picot hem easing in any fullness at top leaving side seams open. Join collar at center back using 3-needle bind-off technique. Sew straight edge of collar to neck edge.

I-Cord trim

With dpns and MC, work 4-st I-Cord (see page 154) until I-Cord reaches from lower edge of right front, around collar and down left front. Cut yarn, leaving a long tail. Sew I-Cord in place.

I-Cord frog closure

With MC, make a 3-st I-Cord (see page 154) 21"/53.5cm in length and foll diagram make frog and sew to left front. With MC, make a 3-st I-Cord 25"/63.5cm in length and foll diagram make frog with a loop for buttonhole and sew to right front. Tie cord into a single knot for button on left side opposite buttonloop.

○ start
● end

diagram for Cord Frog closing

Color Key

▨	MC	chocolate
▨	A	pumpkin
▨	B	cinnamon
▨	C	taupe
☐	D	sage
▨	E	army green
O		beads

chart 1 for Back and Fronts

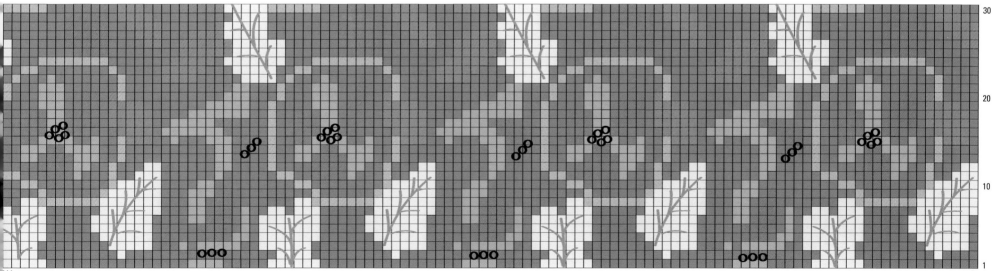

chart 2 for Bell Sleeve

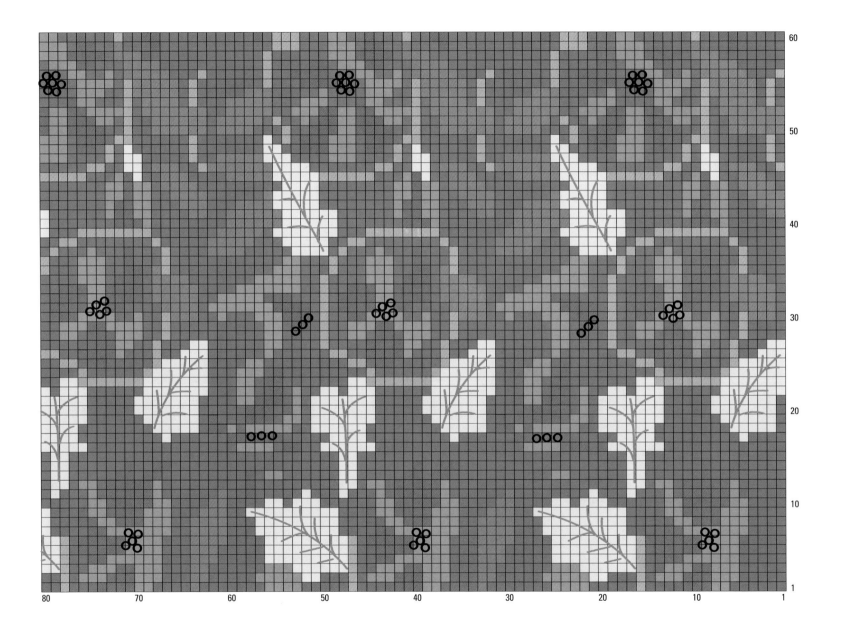

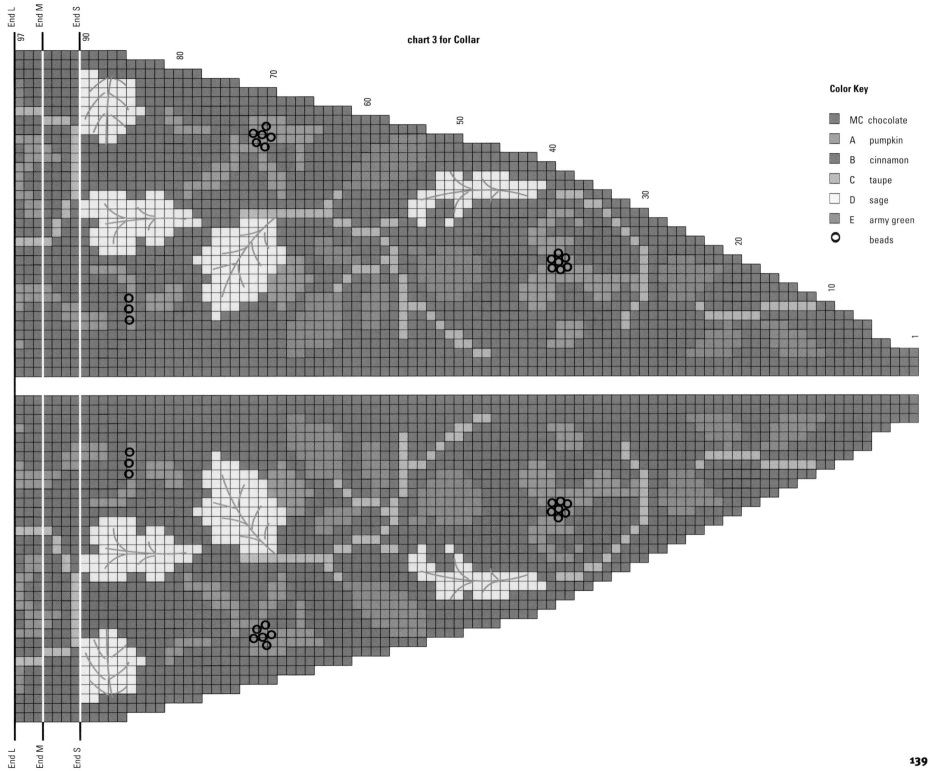

chart 3 for Collar

CARDIGAN WITH CABLED POINTS

SIZES

To fit Small (Medium, Large). Directions are for smallest size with larger sizes in parentheses. If there is only one figure, it applies to all sizes.

KNITTED MEASUREMENTS

- Bust 38 (42, 46)"/ 96.5 (106.5, 116.5)cm
- Length 22 (22½, 23)"/56 (57, 58.5)cm
- Upper arm 13 (14¼, 15½)"/33 (37, 39.5)cm

MATERIALS

- 14 (14, 15) 1¾oz/50g balls (each approx 81yds/74m) of Karabella Supercashmere (100% cashmere) in #716 moss (A) ⑤
- 5 (5, 6) 1¾oz/50g balls (each approx 222yds/203m) of Karabella Gossamer (30% kid mohair/52% nylon/18% polyester) in #6120 mint-silver/gold (B) ④
- One pair size 11 (8mm) needles OR SIZE TO OBTAIN GAUGE
- Three hook and eyes
- Stitch holders

GAUGE

- 14 sts and 18 rows = 4"/10cm over St st using 1 strand each A and B held tog. TAKE TIME TO CHECK GAUGE.

STITCH GLOSSARY

6-st RC Sl 3 sts to cn and hold to back, k3, k3 from cn.

BACK

With 1 strand each A and B held tog, cast on 116 (124, 132) sts.

Beg points

Row 1 (RS) *K12 (13, 14), SKP, k1, k2tog, k12 (13, 14); rep from * to end—108 (116, 124) sts.
Row 2 and all WS rows Purl.
Row 3 *K11 (12, 13), SKP, k1, k2tog, k11 (12, 13); rep from * to end—100 (108, 116) sts.
Row 5 *K10 (11, 12), SKP, k1, k2tog, k10 (11, 12); rep from * to end—92 (100, 108) sts.
Row 7 *K9 (10, 11), SKP, k1, k2tog, k9 (10, 11); rep from * to end—84 (92, 100) sts.
Row 9 *K8 (9, 10), SKP, k1, k2tog, k8 (9, 10); rep from * to end—76 (84, 92) sts.
Row 11 *K7 (8, 9), SKP, k1, k2tog, k7 (8, 9); rep from * to end—68 (76, 84) sts.
Row 13 *K4 (5, 6), p1, k3, k2tog, k2, p1, k4 (5, 6); rep from * to end—64 (72, 80) sts.
Row 14 K the knit sts and p the purl sts.

Beg cables

Rows 1 and 3 (RS) *K4 (5, 6), p1, k6, p1, k4 (5, 6); rep from * to end.
Rows 2, 4 and 6 K the knit sts and p the purl sts.
Row 5 *K4 (5, 6), p1, 6-st RC, p1, k4 (5, 6); rep from * to end.
Rep rows 1-6 twice more.
Cont to work all sts in St st until piece measures 13½"/34.5cm from beg (measured from inside point of V).

Armhole shaping

Bind off 3 sts at beg of next 2 rows, 2 sts at beg of next 2 rows. Dec 1 st each side every other row 3 times—48 (56, 64) sts. Work even until armhole measures 8½ (9, 9½)"/21.5 (23, 24)cm. Bind off.

BACK PANEL LOWER PEPLUM

With 1 strand each of A and B held tog, cast on 116 (124, 132) sts. Work same as back until last cable rep. Bind off.

LEFT FRONT

With 1 strand each A and B held tog, cast on 68 (72, 76) sts.

Beg points

Row 1 (RS) *K12 (13, 14), SKP, k1, k2tog, k12 (13, 14); rep from *, end p2, k6, p2 (for front band)—64 (68, 72) sts.
Row 2 and all WS rows K2, p6, k2, p to end.
Row 3 *K11 (12, 13), SKP, k1, k2tog, k11 (12, 13); rep from *, end p2, k6, p2—60 (64, 68) sts.
Row 5 *K10 (11, 12), SKP, k1, k2tog, k10 (11, 12); rep from *, end p2, 6-st RC, p2—56 (60, 64) sts.
Row 7 *K9 (10, 11), SKP, k1, k2tog, k9 (10, 11); rep from *, end p2, k6, p2—52 (56, 60) sts.
Row 9 *K8 (9, 10), SKP, k1, k2tog, k8 (9, 10); rep from *, end p2, k6, p2—48 (52, 56) sts.
Row 11 *K7 (8, 9), SKP, k1, k2tog, k7 (8, 9); rep from *, end p2, 6-st RC, p2—44 (48, 52) sts.
Row 13 *K4 (5, 6), p1, k3, k2tog, k2, p1, k4 (5, 6); rep from *, end p2, k6, p2—42 (46, 50) sts.
Row 14 Rep row 2.

Beg cables

Row 1 (RS) *K4 (5, 6), p1, k6, p1, k4 (5, 6); rep from *, end p2, k6, p2.
Rows 2, 4 and 6 K the knit sts and p the purl sts.
Row 3 *K4 (5, 6), p1, k6, p1, k4 (5, 6); rep form *, end p2, 6-sts RC, p 2.
Row 5 *K4 (5, 6), p1, 6-st RC, p1, k4 (5, 6); rep from *, end p2, K6, p2.
Rep rows 1–6 twice more.
Cont to work 10 sts at front edge in cable as established and rem sts in St st until piece measures 13½"/34.5cm from beg (measured from inside point of V). Shape armhole at side edge (beg of RS rows) as for back—34 (38, 42) sts. Work even until armhole measures 6 (6½, 7)"/15 (16.5, 18)cm, end with a WS row.

Neck shaping

Next row (RS) Work to last 8 sts, place last 8 sts on a holder for front band.
Next row (WS) Bind off 6 sts (neck edge), work to end. Cont to bind off from neck edge 3 sts once, 2 sts twice, then dec 1 st every other row twice. Work even if necessary until same length as back. Bind off rem 11 (15, 19) sts for shoulder.

RIGHT FRONT

Work same as left front, reversing shaping.

SLEEVES

With 1 strand each of A and B held tog, cast on 45 sts.

Beg Points

Row 1 (RS) K20, SKP, k1, k2tog, k20—43 sts.
Rows 2, 4, 6, 8, 10 and 12 Purl.
Row 3 K19, SKP, k1, k2tog, k19—41 sts.
Row 5 K18, SKP, k1, k2tog, k18—39 sts.
Row 7 K17, SKP, k1, k2tog, k17—37 sts.
Row 8 K16, SKP, k1, k2tog, k16—35 sts.
Row 9 K15, SKP, k1, k2tog, k15—33 sts.
Row 11 K14, SKP, k1, k2tog, k14—31 sts.
Row 13 K11, p1, k3, k2tog, k2, p1, k11—30 sts.
Row 14 and all foll WS rows K the knit sts and p the purl sts.
Rows 15 and 17 K11, p1, k6, p1, k11.
Row 19 K11, p1, 6-st RC, p1, k11.
Cont in pat as established, crossing cable at center every 6th row, AT SAME TIME, inc 1 st each side (working inc sts into St st) on the next RS row, then every 8th (6th, 6th) row 7 (9, 11) times more—46 (50, 54) sts. Work even until piece measures 18"/45.5cm from beg (measure at side edge, not in center).

Cap shaping

Bind off 3 sts at beg of next 2 rows, 2 sts at beg of next 2 rows, dec 1 st each side every other row 6 (7, 8) times. Bind off 3 sts at beg of next 4 rows. Bind off rem 12 (14, 16) sts.

COLLAR

With 1 strand each of A and B held tog, cast on 145 (155, 165) sts. Work same as back, working 14 rows of beg points and 18 rows of beg cables—80 (90, 100) sts. Work in St st for 2 rows. Bind off.

FINISHING

Sew shoulder seams. Set in sleeves. Sew side and sleeve seams. Pin collar in place and sew around neck edge. Sew bound off edge of back panel lower peplum in a half moon shape under back points where cables begin. Sew hook and eyes evenly spaced between neck edge and waist.

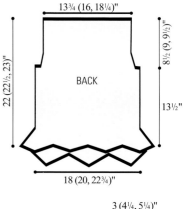

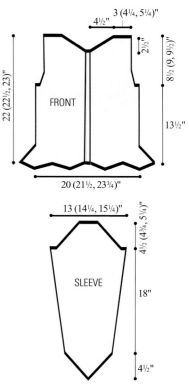

HOODED SHAWL

KNITTED MEASUREMENTS
27½ x 66"/70 x 167.5cm

MATERIALS
- 15 1¾oz/50g skeins (each approx 142yd/130m) of Rowan's RYC Cashsoft DK (57% extra fine Merino wool, 33% microfibre, 10% cashmere) in #512 poppy ③
- One pair size 6 (4mm) needles OR SIZE TO OBTAIN GAUGE
- size 5 (3.75mm) double-pointed needles
- Cable needle (cn)

GAUGE
20 sts and 26 rows = 4"/10cm over St st
TAKE TIME TO CHECK GAUGE.

STITCH GLOSSARY
K1-b Insert needle into the next st in row below, k both loops, drop st off LH needle.

T2L Slip 1 st to cn and hold to front, p1, then k1 tbl from cn.

T2R Slip 1 st to cn and hold to back, k1 tbl, then p1 from cn.

3-st LPC Slip 2 sts to cn and hold to front, p1, then k2 from cn.

3-st RPC Slip 1 st to cn and hold to back, k2, then p1 from cn.

4-st LC Slip 2 sts to cn and hold to front, k2, then k2 from cn.

4-st RC Slip 2 sts to cn and hold to back, k2, then k2 from cn.

5-st LC Slip 3 sts onto cn and hold to front, k2, sl the p st from cn back to LH needle, p this st, then k2 from cn.

5-st RC Slip 3 sts onto cn and hold to back, k2, sl the p st from cn back to LH needle, p this st, then k2 from cn.

MB (make bobble) [K in front, back, front, back and front] of next st—5 sts, turn, p5, turn, k5, turn, p5, turn, k5, then slip the 2nd, 3rd, 4th and 5th st over the first st.

PATTERN I (worked over 14 sts)
Row 1 (RS) P1, k1-b, p1, k8, p1, k1-b, p1.
Row 2 and all WS rows K1, p1, k1, p8, k1, p1, k1.
Row 3 P1, k1-b, p1, 4-st RC, 4-st LC, p1, k1-b, p1.
Row 5 P1, k1-b, p1, k8, p1, k1-b, p1.
Row 7 P1, k1-b, p1, 4-st LC, 4-st RC, p1, k1-b, p1.
Rep rows 1 to 8 for Pat I.

PATTERN II (worked over 9 sts)
Row 1 (RS) P3, [k1 tbl] 3 times, p3.
Row 2 K3, [p1 tbl] 3 times, k3.
Row 3 P2, T2R, k1 tbl, T2L, p2.
Row 4 K2, [p1 tbl , k1] 2 times, p1 tbl, k2.
Row 5 P1, T2R, p1, k1 tbl, p1, T2L, p1.
Row 6 K1, [p1 tbl, k2] 2 times, p1 tbl, k1.
Row 7 T2R, p1, [k1 tbl] 3 times, p1, T2L.
Row 8 P1 tbl, k2, [p1 tbl] 3 times, k2, p1 tbl.
Rep rows 1 to 8 for Pat II.

PATTERN III (worked over 23 sts)
Row 1 (RS) K2, p7, k2, p1, k2, p7, k2.
Row 2 P2, k7, p2, k1, p2, k7, p2.
Row 3 K2, p3, MB, p3, 5-st RPC, p3, MB, p3, k2.
Row 4 Rep row 2.
Row 5 3-st LPC, p5, 3-st RPC, p1, 3-st LPC, p5, 3-st RPC.
Row 6 K1, p2, k5, p2, k3, p2, k5, p2, k1.
Row 7 P1, 3-st LPC, p3, 3-st RPC, p3, 3-st LPC, p3, 3-st RPC, p1.
Row 8 K2, p2, k3, p2, k5, p2, k3, p2, k2.
Row 9 P2, 3-st LPC, p1, 3-st RPC, p5, 3-st LPC, p1, 3-st RPC, p2.

Row 10 K3, p2, k1, p2, k7, p2, k1, p2, k3.
Row 11 P3, 5-st LPC, p7, 5-st LPC, p3.
Row 12 Rep row 10.
Row 13 P2, 3-st RPC, p1, 3-st LPC, p5, 3-st RPC, p1, 3-st LPC, p2.
Row 14 Rep row 8.
Row 15 P1, 3-st RPC, p3, 3-st LPC, p3, 3-st RPC, p3, 3-st LPC, p1.
Row 16 Rep row 6.
Row 17 3-st RPC, p5, 3-st LPC, p1, 3-st RPC p5, 3-st LPC.
Rep rows 2 to 17 for Pat III.

SHAWL Cast on 137 sts (135 sts plus 2 selvedge sts). Work 2 rows in St st.
Est pat Row 1 (RS) K1 (selvedge st), work 8 sts in reverse St st, 14 sts Pat I, 7 sts reverse St st, 9 sts Pat II, 7 sts reverse St st, 3 sts rib, 8 sts reverse St st, 23 sts Pat III, 8 sts reverse St st, 3 sts rib, 7 sts reverse St st, 9 sts Pat II, 7 sts reverse St st, 14 sts Pat I, 8 sts reverse St st, k1 (selvedge st). Cont even in pat as established until piece measures 66"/167.5cm, ending with row 4. Work 2 rows in St st. Bind off.

HOOD
Cast on 76 sts (75 sts plus 1 selvage st). Work 2 rows in St st.
Est pat Row 1 (RS) Beg at neck edge, work 8 sts reverse St st, 14 sts Pat I, 8 sts reverse St st, 3 sts rib, 8 sts reverse St st, 23 sts Pat III, 8 sts reverse St st, 3 sts rib, k1 (selvedge st), end at back edge. Cont even in pat as established until piece meas 24"/61cm, end with row 4. Work 2 rows in St st. Bind off.

FINISHING
Fold hood in half. Sew back seam. Align back seam of hood and center of shawl at neck edge. Sew lower edge of hood to shawl.

I-CORD AND POD TRIM
Pod (worked back and forth in rows)
*Inc row (RS) K in front and back of every st—10 sts.
Purl 1 row.
Rep inc row—20 sts.
Work even in St st for 5 rows.
Dec row (RS) K2tog to end—10 sts.
Purl 1 row.
Rep dec row—5 sts.
Cont in 5-st I-Cord (see page 154) for 3"/7.5cm.*
Long cord (make 2)
Work 5-st I-Cord for 1.5"/3.5cm. Work Pod from * to * 5 times. Bind off.
Short cord (make 2)
Work 5-st I-Cord for 3"/7.5cm. Work Pod from * to * 4 times, end with 1.5"/3.5cm of 5-st I-Cord. Bind off.
Stuff pods with fiberfill and sew seams. Hold cast-on edges of one long and one short cord tog and twist so pods intertwine. Sew

FAUX FAIR ISLE JACKET

one set to each cast-on and bound-off edge.

SIZES
Medium/Large.

KNITTED MEASUREMENTS
- Bust 40"/101.5cm
- Length 24"/61cm (without tabs); 28"/71cm (with tabs)
- Upper arm 17"/43cm

MATERIALS
- 4 1¾oz/50g balls (each approx 101yds/ 92mm) of Jamieson's Heather Aran from Simply Shetland (100% wool) in oceanic #692

(A) 🔢
- 1 ball in #1390 highland mist (B)
- 2 balls in #164 horizon (C)
- 2 balls in #1310 amethyst (D)
- 3 balls in #808 pippin (E)
- 1 ball in #234 pine (F)
- 1 ball in #383 husk (G)
- 1 ball in #1190 burnt umber (H)
- 2 balls in #331 ginger snap (I)
- 2 balls in #1220 lacquer (J)
- One pair each sizes 7 and 8 (4.5 and 5mm) needles OR SIZE TO OBTAIN GAUGE
- Stitch holders

GAUGE
- 20 sts and 20 rows = 4"/10cm over Fair Isle pat in St st on larger needles.
TAKE TIME TO CHECK GAUGE.

LOWER EDGE TABS
Follow Tab Charts a through h. With larger needles, cast on in row 1 color and work 2 rows seed st. With RS facing, beg with row 1 of chart. Make 16 separate tabs (2 of each design). Place on separate holders.

BACK
With RS facing and larger needles, place tabs on LH needle in the foll order: a, b, c, d, e, f, g, h—100 sts.
With RS facing and H, beg with row 1 of Back Extension Chart, work 22 rows in Fair Isle pat.
Cont with row 1 of Back Chart; AT THE SAME TIME, after 80 rows of Back Chart have been completed, bind off 11 sts at beg of next 2 rows for underarm. Bind off on row 123.

LEFT FRONT
With RS facing and larger needles, place tabs on LH needles in the foll order: e, f, g, h— 50 sts.
With RS facing, beg with row 1 of Left Front Chart, work 80 rows in Fair Isle pat. Bind off 11 sts at beg of row 81, then work pat across

neck following chart until 23 sts rem. Bind off rem 23 sts on row 123.

RIGHT FRONT

With RS facing and larger needles, place tabs on LH needle in the foll order: a, b, c, d— 50 sts.

With RS facing, beg with row 1 of Right Front Chart. Work to correspond to left front, reversing all shaping.

SLEEVES

Note Sleeves are worked from the sweater body down. Join shoulder seams.

With RS facing, A and larger needles, pick up 83 sts around sleeve opening. Beg with row 1 of Sleeve Chart, work in Fair Isle pat foll chart dec sequence.

Cuff

Cont with rows 107-123 of Cuff Chart in reverse St st beg with a k row. After Cuff Chart has been completed, cont with 4 rows of Edge Chart in reverse St st, end with a WS row. With A, purl 2 rows, then work 3 rows in St st. Bind off loosely.

COLLAR

With E and larger needles, cast on 3 sts. Beg with row 1 of Collar Chart, work until chart has been completed, taking care to inc and dec where indicated. Bind off rem 3 sts.

Collar edge

With RS facing, larger needles and A, pick up 117 sts along straight edge of collar. Beg on RS, work 4 rows of Edge Chart, end with a WS row. Change to A. Purl 2 rows.

Dec row (RS) K3, k2tog, [k7, k2tog] 12 times, k4. Purl next row. Knit next row. Bind off loosely.

FRONT EDGE

With RS facing, larger needles and A, pick up and k 81 sts along left front edge. Beg on RS, work 4 rows of Edge Chart, end with a WS row. Change to A. Purl 2 rows.

Dec row (RS) K3, k2tog, [k7, k2tog] 8 times, k4.

Purl 1 row. Knit 1 row. Bind off loosely. Rep for right front.

FINISHING

Sew side and sleeve seams. Turn hem of collar and front edges to wrong side and sew in place. Weave in ends. Press lightly.

LOOP BUTTONHOLE AND BUTTON

Loop buttonhole

With A and smaller needles, cast on 6 sts using invisible cast-on (see page 152). Work in St st for 41 rows. Place cast-on sts on needle—12 sts.

Next row (RS) K1, [p1, k1] twice, p2tog, [k1, p1] twice, k1.

Next row *P1, k1; rep from *, end p1. Cont in 1x1 rib for 2 rows more. Bind off in pat.

Button

With A and smaller needles, cast on 6 sts. Work in St st for 24 rows (approx 4"/10cm). Tie in knot. Fold cast-on and bound-off edge to bottom and sew tog. Sew in place on jacket (see Fronts Chart for placement of loop and buttons).

TWISTED LOOP EDGING

Collar

*With A and larger needles, cast on 6 sts using invisible cast-on. Work in St st for 3"/8cm. Cut yarn and leave sts on needle. On same needle, rep from * to make 20 strips total.

To join strips

K6, *bring cast-on edge of just-worked strip behind next strip, using 3-needle joining technique (see page 152), k the 6 sts from these 2 strips tog to form loop; rep from *, end k6 from cast-on edge of last strip. Purl 1 row. K 1 row. Bind off. Sew to edge of collar.

Cuffs (make 2)

Work same as collar beg with 10 strips. Sew to edges of cuffs.

Embroidery

Following Fronts and Back charts, embroider patterns. (For embroidery stitch diagrams see page 153).

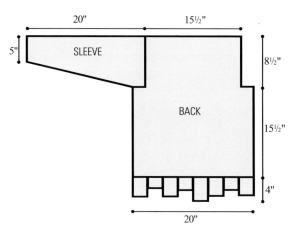

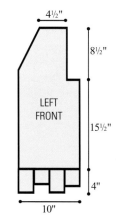

Color Key

- A oceanic
- B highland mist
- C horizon
- D amethyst
- E pippin
- F pine
- G husk
- H burnt umber
- I ginger snap
- J laquer

back extension chart

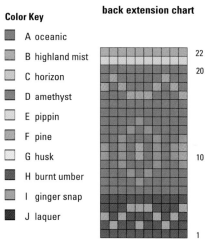

10 sts

tab charts

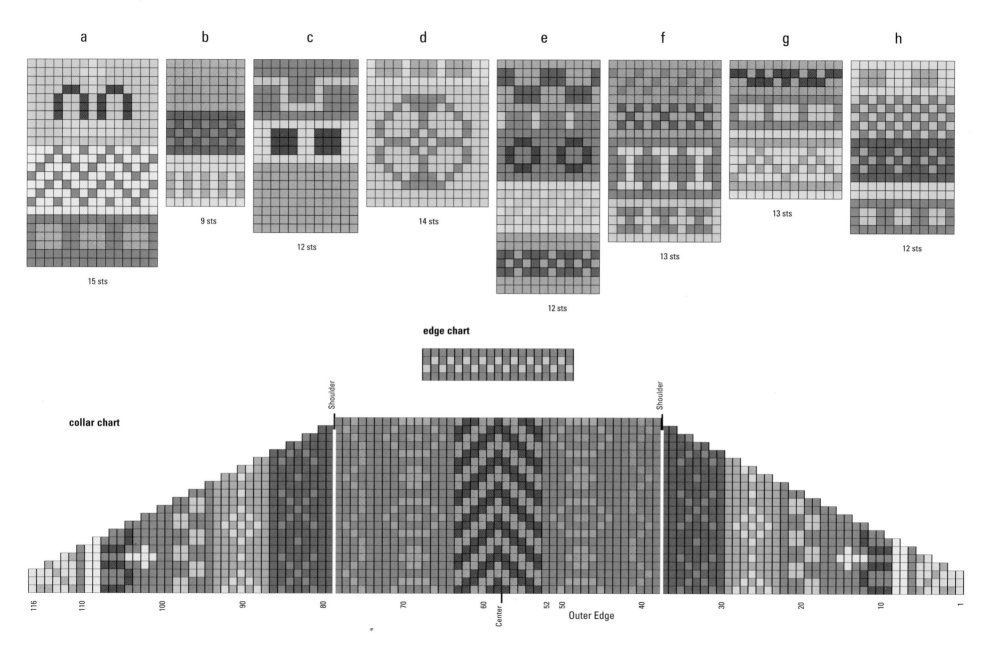

a

15 sts

b

9 sts

c

12 sts

d

14 sts

e

12 sts

f

13 sts

g

13 sts

h

12 sts

edge chart

collar chart

Shoulder

Shoulder

116 110 100 90 80 70 60 52 50 40 30 20 10 1

Center

Outer Edge

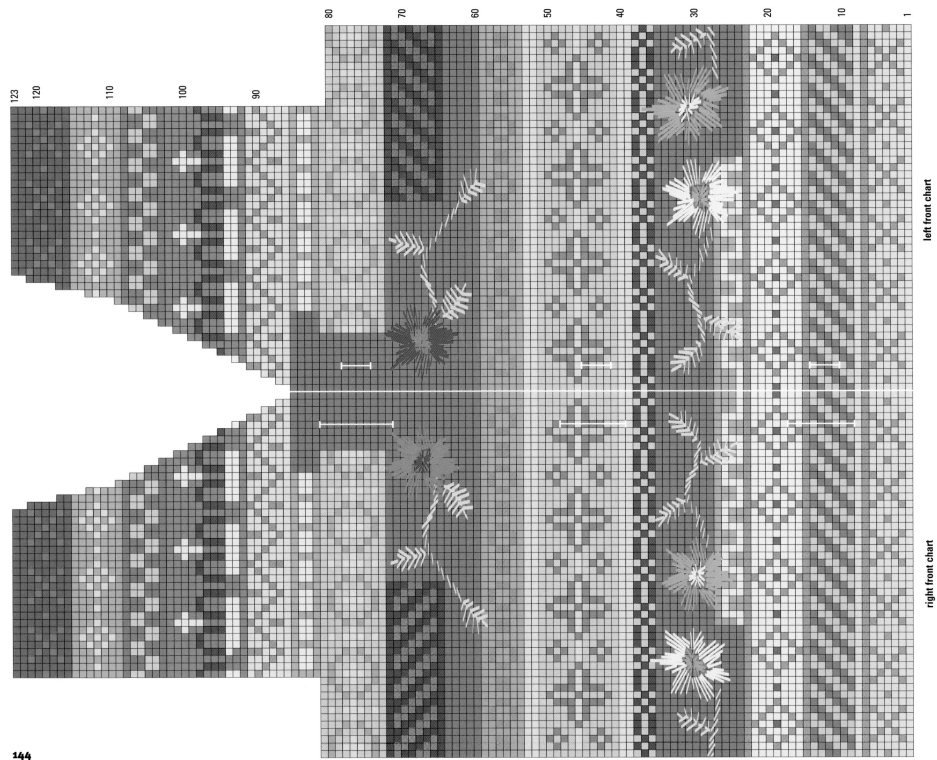

left front chart

right front chart

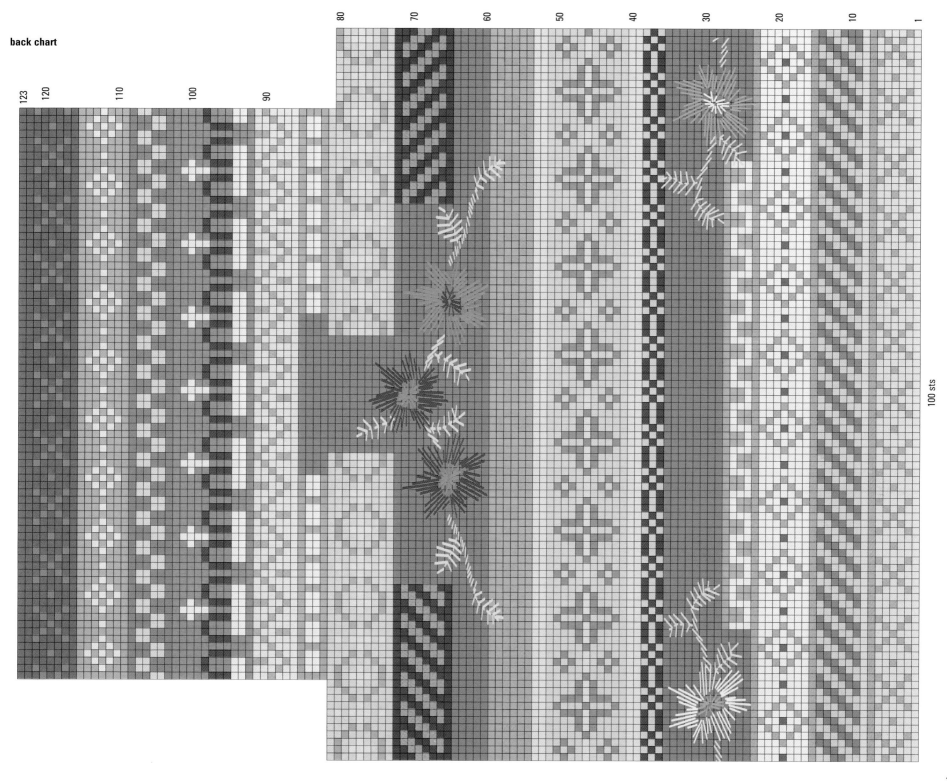

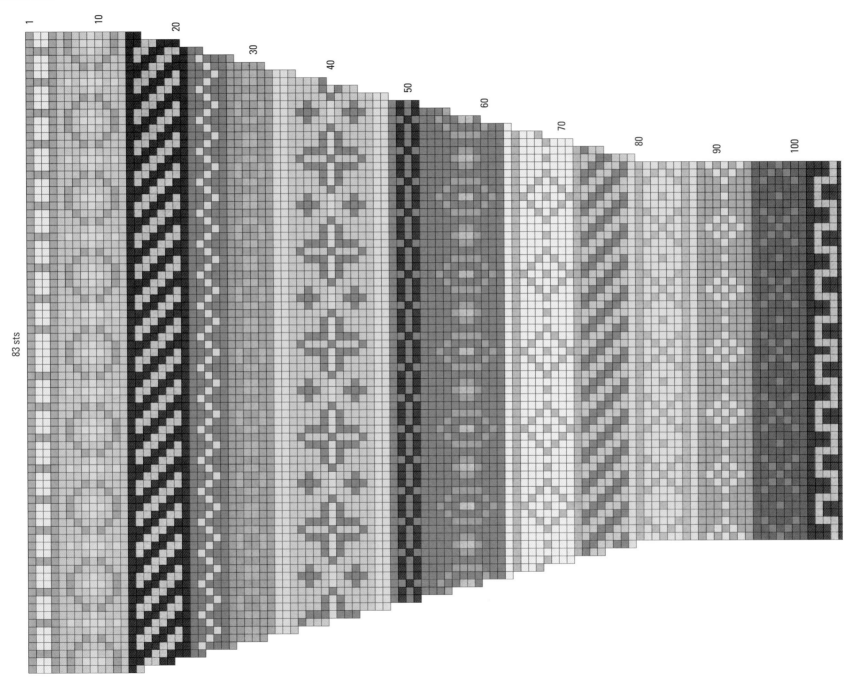

83 sts

cuff chart

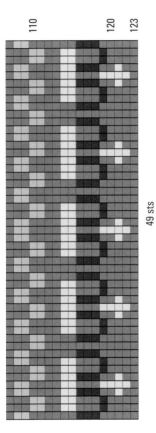

110   120 123

49 sts

DEEP V-NECK SLEEVELESS SWEATER

From page 55

SIZES

To fit Small (Medium, Large). Directions are for smallest size with larger sizes in parentheses. If there is only one figure, it applies to all sizes.

KNITTED MEASUREMENTS

- Bust 36 (40, 44)"/91.5 (101.5, 111.5)cm
- Length 20 (20½, 21)"/51 (52, 53)cm

MATERIALS

- 4 (5, 6) 1¾oz/50g balls (each approx 222yds/ 203mm) of Karabella Gossamer (30% kid mohair/52% nylon/18% polyester) in #6090 lilac **④**
- One pair size 5 (3.75mm) needles OR SIZE TO OBTAIN GAUGE
- Size 5 (3.75mm) circular needle, 24"/60cm long
- Stitch markers

GAUGE

- 14 sts and 18 rows = 4"/10cm over St st. TAKE TIME TO CHECK GAUGE

BACK

With straight needles, cast on 63 (71, 77) sts.

Work in St st until piece measures 12"/30.5cm from beg, end with a WS row. Place a marker at each end of last row for armhole. Work even until armhole measures 8 (8½, 9)"/20.5 (21.5, 23)cm above markers. Bind off.

FRONT

Work as for back until piece measures 7"/18cm from beg, end with a WS row.

Deep V-neck

Next row (RS) K31 (35, 38), join a 2nd ball of yarn and bind off center st, k to end. Working both sides at once, dec 1 st at each neck edge every other row 15 times—16 (20, 23) sts rem for each shoulder. AT THE SAME TIME, when piece measures 12" from beg, place a marker at each end of last row for armhole. Work even until armhole measures 8 (8½, 9)"/20.5 (21.5, 23) cm above markers. Bind off.

FINISHING

Block pieces to measurements. Sew shoulder seams. Sew side seams to armhole markers.

Neck ruffle

With circular needle, cast on 100 (105, 110) sts. Do not join. K 1 row. Inc 1 st in each st on next row—200 (210, 220) sts. K 1 row. Inc 1 st in each st on next row—400 (420, 440)

sts. K 2 rows. Bind off knitwise.

Beg at V-neck on front, sew cast-on edge of ruffle up right front neck, around back neck and down left front neck easing in to fit.

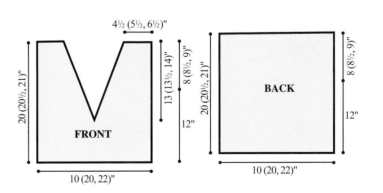

4½ (5½, 6½)"

13 (13½, 14)"

8 (8½, 9)"

20 (20½, 21)"

12"

FRONT

10 (20, 22)"

20 (20½, 21)"

8 (8½, 9)"

BACK

12"

10 (20, 22)"

147

Here is a sampling of neck shapes used throughout this book. Below each neck are the instructions for the neck shaping, based on a worsted-weight yarn with a gauge of 18 sts and 26 rows to 4"/10cm and a cross back (shoulder to shoulder) measurement of 14", with the neck being 6" wide and varying neck drops. These are standard neck shapes upon which you can add most of the edgings shown in this book. It may be necessary in some cases to adjust the number of stitches in the neck to accommodate the stitch multiples of a particular pattern.

Altering the neck

These standard neck sizes do not work for everyone. Let's say your gauge is 4 sts and 6 rows to 1" and you want the width of a V-neck to be 7" and the depth to be 6". First calculate the number of stitches in total for the neck, therefore 7" x 4 sts = 28 sts. Then determine the number of rows for the neck drop—6" x 6 rows = 36 rows. Assuming that your cross back remains 14", then 14" x 4 sts = 56 sts. Because your neck is an even number of sts, you simply divide the work in half to continue the neck shaping, therefore work 28 sts, join a 2nd ball of yarn and work to end. Divide the number of neck stitches in half to determine how many neck decreases must be worked—28 sts divided by two = 14 stitches to decrease in 36 rows. It is best to

have at least an inch worked even at the top of neck before binding off for shoulders, so take 6 rows from the 36 to equal 30 rows. Then divide 30 rows by 14 neck decreases which equals 2.1428…. In other words, if you decrease 1 st every 2nd row 14 times you will get 28 rows, which works out perfectly.

Fitting a neckline into a given neck edge

If you are using the neck shaping as given in the instructions, and want to slot one of these necklines into it, you will have to determine how many stitches to pick up around the neck. If the pattern calls for a specific number of stitches, you may be able to just use that number. However, if the collar needs to be a particular repeat, such as 10 stitches, and the number of stitches to pick up is 96, then pick up this number and adjust the stitches on the first row. In this case, the closest multiple to 10 is 100 stitches, so you would need to increase 4 sts on the first row to come up to 100 stitches. This holds true with cuffs and front borders as well. You may have to increase or decrease stitches from the original pattern to accommodate the repeat.

If the difference in stitches is much larger than 5 or 6 sts because of a very large repeat, you many not want to adjust the number of stitches so dramatically as to

distort the finished edge. Let's say the repeat is over 20 sts and the instructions call for 110 stitches to be picked up. Adjusting the stitches by 10 either way may be too many, so find the closest number to a full repeat, which would be 100, and divide the difference by two, that is 5 sts which can be worked each side as plain stitches.

How many stitches to pick up

Many times the instructions will tell you how many stitches to pick up around a neck or along a front edge. If they do not, or if you have changed the length or width measurement from the original, you will have to recalculate the number. It is easiest along a straight edge. With the garment laying flat, measure the edge, then multiply that measurement by the stitch gauge of the border (you may have to swatch the border pattern if you do not know the gauge). When working around a neck, it is harder to measure a curve. The rule of thumb for a curved neck is to pick up 1 stitch in every bound-off stitch and 3 sts for every 4 rows (for a light to medium weight yarn) or 2 sts for every 3 rows (for a worsted to heavy weight yarn). You can then adjust the number of stitches after the picked up row to accommodate the repeat of the stitch pattern.

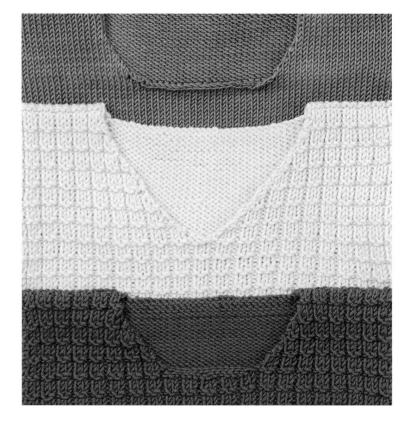

round neck

Beg with 63 sts.

Work in St st for 5½"/14cm, end with a WS row.

Next row (RS) K25, join a 2nd ball of yarn and bind off center 13 sts, k to end.

Working both sides at once, bind off 2 sts at each neck edge once, then dec 1 st each neck edge every other row 5 times—18 sts rem for each shoulder. Work even until piece measures 2½"/6.5cm above bound-off center sts. Bind off. Sew shoulder seams.

(page 71)

scoop neck

Beg with 63 sts.

Work in St st for 4"/10cm, end with a WS row.

Next row (RS) K20, join a 2nd ball of yarn and bind off center 23 sts, k to end.

Working both sides at once, bind off 2 sts at each neck edge once—18 sts rem for each shoulder. Work even until piece measures 4"/10cm above bound-off center sts. Bind off. Sew shoulder seams.

(page 63)

v-neck

Beg with 63 sts.

Work in St st for 3"/7.5cm, end with a WS row.

Next row (RS) K31, join a 2nd ball of yarn and bind off center st, k to end.

Working both sides at once, dec 1 st each side every 4th row 13 times as foll: k1, ssk, k to last 3 sts, k2tog, k1—18 sts rem for each shoulder. Work until piece measures 5"/12.5cm above dividing row. Bind off. Sew shoulder seams.

(page 67)

deep v-neck

Beg with 63 sts.

Work in St st for 1"/2.5cm, end with a WS row.

Next row (RS) K31, join a 2nd ball of yarn and bind off center st, k to end.

Working both sides at once, dec 1 st each side every other row 13 times—18 sts rem for each shoulder. Work even until piece measures 7"/18cm above dividing row. Bind off. Sew shoulder seams.

(page 55)

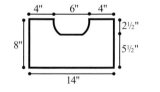

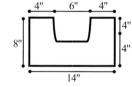

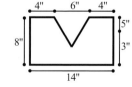

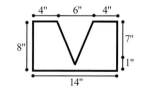

shawl collar

With RS facing and circular needle, pick up sts along right front, pm for start of neck shaping, pick up sts around neck, pm at end of neck shaping, pick up sts down left front. Work in garter st for 9 rows, making button-holes on 5th row of right front.

Short rows

Knit to within 2 sts of 2nd neck marker, wrap and turn (w&t) as foll: sl 1, bring yarn to front, sl same st back to LH needle, turn work. Knit to within last 2 sts before next marker, w&t. Rep last 2 rows 3 more times, working 2 less sts each time.

Next row Knit across row, knitting wrap at every short row tog with corresponding st on needle. Knit all sts on last row, knitting wrap with corresponding st on needle.

Bind off.

Sew buttons opposite buttonholes.

(page 70)

boat neck

Cast on 63 sts.

Work in St st for 7"/17.5cm, end with a WS row.

Next row (RS) K15, join a 2nd ball of yarn, work 33 sts in 1x1 rib, k to end.

Working both sides at once, work first 15 and last 15 sts in St st and center 33 sts in 1x1 rib for 1"/2.5cm. Bind off. Sew shoulder seams.

(page 66)

placket neck

Cast on 63 sts.

Work in St st for 2"/5cm, end WS row.

Next row (RS) K27, join a 2nd ball of yarn and bind off center 9 sts, k to end.

Work both sides at once until piece measures 6"/15cm.

Shape neck

Bind off 4 sts at each neck edge once, then dec 1 st at each neck edge every row 5 times—18 sts rem each shoulder. Work even until piece measures 6"/15cm above bound-off center sts. Bind off. Sew shoulder seams.

First placket With RS facing, pick up 30 sts along pullover front neck opening.

Rows 1 and 3 (WS) P2, *k2, p2; rep from * to end.

Rows 2 and 6 K2, *p2, k2; rep from * to end.

Row 4 (buttonhole row) K2, *p2tog, yo, k2, p2, k2; rep from *, end p2tog, yo, k2.

Rows 5 and 7 Rep row 1.

Row 8 Bind off in rib.

Second placket Work same as first placket along other side of front neck opening, omit-ting buttonholes on Row 4.

Sew edge of plackets across front neck bound-off sts.

(page 68)

PATTERNS

dot stitch

(multiple of 4 sts plus 3)

Row 1 (RS) K1, *p1, k3; rep from *, end p1, k1.

Row 2 Purl.

Row 3 *K3, p1; rep from *, end k3.

Row 4 Purl.

Rep rows 1–4.

waffle stitch

(multiple of 3 sts plus 1)

Rows 1 and 3 (RS) P1, *k2, p1; rep from * to end.

Row 2 K1, *p2, k1; rep from * to end.

Row 4 Purl.

Rep rows 1–4.

beaded rib

(multiple of 2 sts)

Row 1 (RS) *P1, k1; rep from * to end.

Row 2 Purl.

Rep rows 1 and 2.

mistaken rib

(multiple of 4 sts plus 3)

Row 1 *K2, p2; rep from *, end k2, p1.

Rep row 1.

twin rib

(multiple of 6 sts)

Row 1 *K3, p3; rep from * to end.

Row 2 *K1, p1; rep from * to end.

Rep rows 1 and 2.

mock rib

(multiple of 2 sts plus 1)

Row 1 (RS) K1, *p1, k1; rep from * to end.

Row 2 P1, *sl 1 wyif, p1; rep from * to end.

Rep rows 1 and 2.

Let's say that you want to use one of the button band edges on one of your favorite sweater patterns, but the instructions you have are for a pullover. Using these simple steps, you can turn the one front of the pullover into two pieces: left and right front. Most pattern booklets these days are accompanied by schematic drawings of the different pieces. These illustrations are drawn to scale and show you not only the shape of these pieces, but also crucial measurements that can be used when altering a pattern.

We are giving an example here of a pullover which is 20" wide at the lower edge and bust, has a crewneck, and the gauge is 18 sts and 26 rows = 4" (or 4.5 sts and 6.5 rows - 1"). We will show you how to make this pullover into a V-neck cardigan. First you need to know how wide the center front band will be. In our example it is 2" wide. Subtract this 2" from the lower edge measurement, therefore 20" - 2" = 18 ". Divide this result in half (as you need two equal sections for the front); 18" divided by 2" = 9", which will be the new measurement for each front. Multiply 9" x 4.5 (your stitch gauge) to get the total number of stitches to cast on = 40.5 sts. Round this number up or down a few stitches, depending on the stitch pattern multiple that you are using for the body. In our exam-

ple we will use 4 plus 2 (divide 4 into 40 = 10). Then add 2 which equals 42 sts for the body. Now we will need to adjust this number to accommodate the edging pattern multiple that you have chosen. Our example will be an edging with a multiple of 9 + 2. Since 42 is not an exact multiple of 9 + 2, you must find the nearesy multiple, which in this case would be: 9 x 5 = 45 + 2 = 47 sts to cast on. When edging pattern is completed, decrease 5 sts evenly across the next row to obtain the 42 sts needed for the body pattern.

Work the pattern to the underarm. In this case, we have the V-neck shaping beginning at the same place as the armhole shaping. Therefore, you need to do a little bit of math before continuing. First determine how many stitches were bound-off on the back on one side, in this case it was 9 sts. Subtract this from the total number of sts (42 - 9 = 33). Now determine how many stitches for the shoulder: 4½" x 4.5 = 20.25, rounded down to 20 sts. Therefore, 33 - 20 = 13 sts which is the number of sts you need to decrease at the neck. Since the neck drop is 8" long, 8 x 6.5 (the row gauge) = 52 rows. Divide 52 by 13 and you get 4. So in shaping the neck, you dec 1 st at the neck edge on the first row of armhole shaping, then continue the neck decrease every 4th row 12 times more, and

remember to work the same armhole decreases at the side edge only (beg of RS rows for the left front, end of RS rows for the right front) as on the back.

You may want to draw your own schematic with your new measurements onto square graph paper. It is easy enough to do if you know that every square equals one inch. Then on this schematic you can place all your new numbers, as we have shown here.

Now you need to pick up stitches along the front edges for the button and buttonhole bands. For pointers on a smooth pick up, see "How many stitches to pick up" on page 148. Be sure that you have the correct multiple for the desired edging. If you calculate that you should pick up 100 stitches, and the edging has a multiple of 5 sts plus 4, then opt for going up to 104 sts. It is better to have a few more sts then a few less.

When figuring the number of buttons you need, be sure that there is not too much space between the buttons. The average distance in between is about 3", with the first and last ones about ½"–1" from each end, but this will vary depending on the size of the buttons, gauge of the yarn, and style of the garment. It is easiest to place markers on the

button band first, then work the buttonholes opposite the markers. Let's say, for example, the buttonband is 16" long. Place makers for the first and last ones ½" from each end. This leaves 15" for the other buttons. If you have 3" in between, then 15" divided by 3" equals 5, therefore, 5 + the 2 each end = 7 buttons in total. The acutal number between the buttons will be a little less then 3", as the size of the button will determine how many stitches to bind off for the buttonhole.

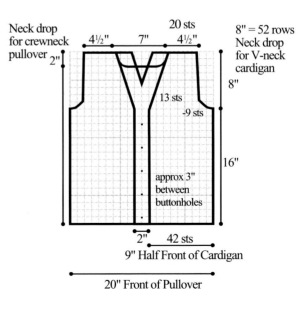

3-needle joining technique Work sts of both layers tog, using 3-needle joining technique as foll: with RS of layers facing (top layer over bottom layer) and the needles parallel, insert a third needle into the first st on each needle and work them tog.

approx approximately

beg begin(ning)

bind off Used to finish an edge and keep stitches from unraveling. Lift the first stitch over the second, the second over the third, etc. (UK: cast off)

cable cast-on Work same as **knit on cast-on**, but after casting on 2 stitches, insert the right needle in between the first two stitches on the left needle, instead of into the first stitch.

cast-on A foundation row of stitches placed on the needle in order to begin knitting.

CC contrast color

cm centimeter(s)

cn cable needle

cont continu(e)(ing)

DD Sl 2 sts tog knitwise, k1, pass 2 sl sts over k st—2 sts dec

dec decrease(ing)—Reduce the stitches in a row (knit 2 together).

dpn double pointed needle(s)

foll follow(s)(ing)

g gram(s)

garter stitch Knit every row. Circular knitting: knit one round, then purl one round.

inc increase(ing)—Add stitches in a row (knit into the front and back of a stitch).

invisible (invisibly) cast-on Cut a strand of contrasting waste yarn approximately four times the required width. With the working yarn, make a slip knot and the needle. Hold the waste yarn beside the slip knot and *take the working yarn under it and over the needle from front to back. Bring the working yarn in front of the waste yarn. Keeping the waste yarn under the needle, repeat from the * until the required number of stitches is cast on. Remove the waste yarn only when the piece is finished.

k knit

k2tog knit 2 stitches together

knit on cast-on Place a slip knot on left-hand needle, leaving a short tail. *Insert the right-hand needle knitwise into the stitch on left-hand needle. Wrap the yarn around the right-hand needle as if to knit. Draw yarn through the first stitch to make a new stitch, but do not drop the stitch from the left needle. Slip the new stitch to the left needle. Repeat from the * until the required number of stitches is cast on.

lp(s) loop(s)

LH left-hand

m meter(s)

M1 make one stitch—With the needle tip, lift the strand between last stitch worked and next stitch on the left-hand needle and knit into the back of it. One stitch has been added.

M1 p-st make one purl stitch—Work same as M1, but purl into back of strand.

make bobble Cast on 1 st. K in front, back, front, back and front again of st (5 sts made in one st). Turn. K 1 row, p 1 row, k 1 row. **Next Row** P2tog, p1, p2tog—3 sts. K 1 row. P3tog, fasten off.

MC main color

p purl

p2 (p3) (p5) tog purl 2 (3) (5) stitches together

pat pattern

pick up and knit (purl) Knit (or purl) into the loops along an edge.

pm place marker—Place or attach a loop of contrast yarn or purchased stitch marker as indicated.

psso pass slipped stitch over

p2sso pass 2 slipped stitches over

rem remain(s)(ing)

rep repeat

rev St st reverse Stockinette stitch—Purl right-side rows, knit wrong-side rows. Circular knitting: purl all rounds. (UK: reverse stocking stitch)

rnd(s) round(s)

RH right-hand

RS right side(s)

sc single crochet (UK: dc - double crochet)

single cast-on Place a slip knot on right-hand needle, leaving a short tail. Wrap yarn from ball around your left thumb from front to back and secure it in your palm with other fingers. Insert needle upwards through the strand on your thumb. Slip this loop from your thumb onto the needle, pulling the yarn from the ball to tighten it. Continue in this way until all the stitches are cast on.

S2KP Sl 2 sts tog, k1, pass the 2 sl sts over the k1—2 sts dec.

SKP Slip 1, knit 1, pass slip stitch over knit 1.

SK2P Slip 1, knit 2 together, pass slip stitch over k2tog.

sl slip—An unworked stitch made by passing a stitch from the left-hand to the right-hand needle as if to purl.

SP2P Sl 1 knitwise, p2tog, psso.

ssk slip, slip, knit—Slip next 2 stitches knitwise, one at a time, to right-hand needle. Insert tip of left-hand needle into fronts of these stitches from left to right. Knit them together. One stitch has been decreased.

spp Slip 1, purl 1, pass slip stitch over purl 1.

st(s) stitch(es)

St st Stockinette stitch—Knit right-side rows, purl wrong-side rows. Circular knitting: knit all rounds. (UK: stocking stitch)

St st cord Cast on 3, 4, 5 or 6 stitches. Row 1 K3, 4, 5 or 6, do not turn, slide sts to other end of needle. Rep row 1 for desired length.

tbl through back of loop

tog together

w&t wrap and turn

WS wrong side(s)

wyib with yarn in back

wyif with yarn in front

work even Continue in pattern without increasing or decreasing. (UK: work straight)

yd yard(s)

yo yarn over—Make a new stitch by wrapping the yarn over the right-hand needle. (UK: yfwd, yon, yrn)

* Repeat directions following * as many times as indicated.

[ ] Repeat directions inside brackets as many times as indicated.

s t i t c h e s

kitchener stitch

1 Insert tapestry needle purlwise (as shown) through first stitch on front needle. Pull yarn through, leaving that stitch on knitting needle.

2 Insert tapestry needle knitwise (as shown) through first stitch on back needle. Pull yarn through, leaving stitch on knitting needle.

3 Insert tapestry needle knitwise through first stitch on front needle, slip stitch off needle and insert tapestry needle purlwise (as shown) through next stitch on front needle. Pull yarn through, leaving this stitch on needle.

4 Insert tapestry needle purlwise through first stitch on back needle. Slip stitch off needle and insert tapestry needle knitwise (as shown) through next stitch on back needle. Pull yarn through, leaving this stitch on needle.

Repeat steps 3 and 4 until all stitches on both front and back needles have been grafted. Fasten off and weave in end.

duplicate stitch

embroidery stitches

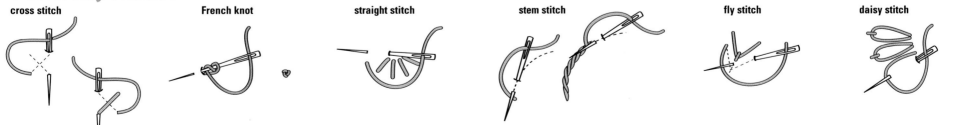

cross stitch   **French knot**   **straight stitch**   **stem stitch**   **fly stitch**   **daisy stitch**

techniques

BASIC BUTTONHOLES

Simple two row buttonhole

Work to buttonhole placement. Bind off desired number of sts for button size (generally 2–4 sts). Finish row.

On next row, work to bound off sts. Using the single cast on method, cast on same number of stitches as were bound off, complete row. On the next row, work the cast on sts through the back loop to tighten them.

Horizontal buttonhole

Work to buttonhole placement. Bind off 1 less than the required number of stitches for your buttonhole size. Slip last st on right hand needle back to left hand needle and knit it together with next stitch, complete row. On next row, work to bound off stitches, cast on one more stitch than was bound off, complete row.

Next row work to one stitch before the extra cast on stitch, knit two together.

One row horizontal buttonhole

Work to buttonhole placement, bring yarn to front and slip a stitch purlwise, bring yarn to back and leave it there. *Slip next stitch from left needle. Pass the first slipped stitch over it; repeat from * until required number of stitches have been bound off. Slip the last stitches back to left needle and turn work. Use the cable cast on with yarn at the back cast on one more stitch than the number bound off, turn work. Slip the first stitch with the yarn in back, from the left needle and pass the extra cast on stitch over it to close the buttonhole, complete the row.

One stitch round buttonhole

Work to buttonhole placement, yo, k2tog, complete the row.

Next row work in pattern.

Two stitch round buttonhole

Work to one stitch before the two stitches designated for buttonhole, k2tog, yo twice, ssk, complete the row.

Next row work to yo's, p in front of 1st yo, p in back of 2nd yo, complete row.

Vertical buttonhole

Divide work at base of buttonhole and work each side separately for the needed row amount to get height for button size. Both sections must end on same row, then rejoin the sections.

Cord Button

Cast on 3, 4 or 5 sts. Work knit cord for approx 3"/7.5cm. Bind off. Tie once, then fold down and sew bound-off edge to cast-on edge. Sew button in place.

Le Fleur

Cast on 35 sts.
Row 1 (WS) *K1, bind off 5 (2 sts on RH needle); rep from * to end—10 sts.
Run threaded tapestry needle through rem sts on needle, pull tightly and secure.

MAKING CORDS

I-Cord

Cast on 3 sts or number of stitches required.
Row 1 K3, do not turn, slide sts to other end of needle.
Rep Row 1 to desired length. Bind off.

Tips

When making cords, use two double-pointed needles or one short circular needle, unless otherwise indicated. The cords are made separately, then sewn on to piece to form the edging. If you sew on the cord, use a tapestry needle and the same yarn used to make the cord. Pin the cord in place on top of the fabric. Use small running stitches, work from the wrong side, catching the cord with each stitch.

RIB FLAP LOVE KNOTS

Slip all strips onto left needle with right side facing you. Working on first two strips only, and always keeping right side facing, cross first strip in front of second strip, then bring cast-on edge of second strip up in front of first strip and tuck it between the two strips and behind the first. Work first 7 stitch of rib pat across sts of first strip and at the same time, on the knit sts only, catch in every other cast-on st of second strip. Next, tuck remainder of cast-on edge of first strip behind sts of second strip, pin and work the next 7 sts of rib pat across these sts, catching in every other cast-on st of first strip, on the knit sts only, thus completing the knot. Work remaining knots in the same way, continuing in rib pat.
Note Strips can be made with contrasting colors.

ROUNDED EDGE

Using increases

Cast on the number of stitches needed minus approximately 18 sts (or 4") for a DK weight yarn.

Note This number will vary if using a different weight yarn. Work in stockinette stitch, casting on sts at beg of RS rows (or WS rows, depending on which side you want the curve as follows: 4 sts twice, 3 sts once, 2 sts twice, 1 st 3 times. This method gives an rather uneven edge, but when picking up the sts around the curve, you can hide this edge.

Using short rows

Cast on the number of stitches needed. You will work the curve over approximately 16 sts (or 4") for a worsted weight yarn.

Note This number will vary if using a different weight yarn. Work in stockinette stitch for 2 rows. Work short rows as foll:
Next row (RS) K16, work wrap & turn (w&t) as foll: sl 1, bring yarn to front, sl same st back to LH needle, turn work; p to end. **Next row (RS)** K13 sts, w&t, p to end. **Next row (RS)** K10 sts, w&t, p to end. **Next row (RS)** K8 sts, w&t, p to end. **Next row (RS)** K6 sts, w&t, p to end. **Next row (RS)** K4 sts, w&t, p to end. **Next row (RS)** K2 sts, w&t, p to end. K all sts, working the wrapped st at every short row tog with corresponding st on needle. Continue as desired. This method gives a smooth edge, for an easy pick up.

a c k n o w l e d g m e n t s

Thank you, as always, to the staff at Sixth&Spring for their support and logistical skills: Trisha Malcolm, Carla Scott, Erica Smith, Erin Walsh, Tanis Gray, Sheena Thomas, Phyllis Howe, and Lillian Esposito.

A special thank you to my art director Chi Ling Moy, who exceeded my wishes to make this book even more beautiful than its predecessors.

Big thank you to Jack Deutsch (photographer extraordinaire) and his staff for the glorious photography.

An affectionate thank you to my devoted, intrepid knitters: Eileen Curry, Nancy Henderson, Dianne Weitzul, and Veronica Manno.

A grateful thank you to Arthur Karapetyan and Rachel Greenstein at Karabella Yarns for their kindness and generosity in supplying yarn for this project, along with Simply Shetland, Muench, and Rowan Yarns. Thanks to Barbara and Jay Barr and Lynita Haber at JHB Buttons for graciously supplying the buttons.

Thanks for the ongoing support from my friends—Jo Brandon, Emily Brenner, Vincent Caputo, Wendy Chung, Rita Greenfeder, Chris Kitch, Leigh Merrifield, and Jenni Stone—in spite of my unreturned phone calls due to deadlines.

A very special thank you to my readers, my students, designers, knitters and yarn shop owners around the world, who have so enthusiastically embraced my work that has kept me on…over…and beyond the edge.

notes

resources

GGH
Distributed by Muench Yarns, Inc.

Jaimeson's
Distributed by Simply Shetland

Karabella Yarns
1201 Broadway
New York, NY 10001
www.karabellayarns.com

Muench Yarns, Inc.
1323 Scott Street
Petaluma, CA 94954-1135
www.myyarn.com

Rowan Yarns
Distributed in the US by Westminster Fibers, Inc.
Distributed in the UK:
Green Lane Mill
Holmfirth
HD9 2DX England
www.knitrowan.com

Simply Shetland
10 Domingo Road
Santa Fe, NM 87508
www.simplyshetland.net

Westminster Fibers
4 Townsend West, Unit 8
Nashua, NH 03063
www.westminsterfibers.com